Ode to
Bass & Trout

An Illustrated Treasury of the Best Angling Literature

"There will be days when the fishing is better

than one's most optimistic forecast, others when it is far worse.

Either is a gain over just staying home."

—Roderick Haig-Brown

Ode to
Bass & Trout

An Illustrated Treasury of the Best Angling Literature

Edited by Alan James Robinson

Illustrations by
Adriano Manocchia, Rock Newcomb, Alan James Robinson,
Joseph Sulkowski, Mark Susinno, and Paco Young

SMITHMARK

Design & Compilation © 1999 Lionheart Books, Ltd.
All artwork Copyrighted to the individual artists:
Adriano Manocchia © pages 9, 16, 28, 44, 50, 52, 74, 80, 89, 95, 96, 117, 125, 142, 152, 154
Rock Newcomb © pages 98, 104, 105, 109, 110, 141, 150
Alan James Robinson © pages 7, 12, 15, 20, 22, 24, 26, 27, 30, 33, 36, 37, 40, 41, 42,46, 49, 60, 71, 73, 76, 77, 84, 85,
94, 100, 102, 106, 108, 124 ,126, 134, 145, 147, 148, 149, 156, 157, 158
Joseph Sulkowski © pages 64, 93, 114, 128, 136, 138
Mark Susinno © pages 18, 21, 35, 38, 42, 55, 58, 63, 66, 78, 82, 86, 103, 107, 118, 122,127, 132, 144
Paco Young © pages 91, 120, 131

This edition published in 1999 by SMITHMARK Publishers,
a division of U.S. Media Holdings, Inc., 115 West 18th Street, New York, NY 10011.

SMITHMARK books are available for bulk purchase for sales promotion and premium use.
For details write or call the manager of special sales, SMITHMARK Publishers,
115 West 18th Street, New York, NY 10011, (212) 519-1300.

Ode to Bass & Trout
was produced by Lionheart Books, Ltd.,
5105 Peachtree Industrial Blvd., Atlanta, Georgia 30341

Design: Carley Wilson Brown
Cover Art: "Duped—Brown Trout"–Mark Susinno

ISBN: 0-7651-0909-3

Printed in Hong Kong

10 9 8 7 6 5 4 3 2 1

Library of Congress Cataloging-in-Publication Data

Ode to bass & trout : an illustrated treasury of the best angling
literature / edited by Alan James Robinson : illustrations by
Adriano Manocchia . . . [et al .] .
    p.   cm.
ISBN: 0-7651-0909-3 (alk. paper)
    1. Bass fishing. 2. Trout fishing.   I. Robinson, Alan James.
II. Title: Ode to bass and trout. III. Title: Bass and trout.
SH681.034   1999
799.1'73--dc21   98-47631
                                                  CIP

TABLE

of CONTENTS

Ode to BASS *&* TROUT—Reprint Acknowledgments

We have made every effort to determine original sources and locate copyright holders
of the excerpts in this book. Grateful acknowledgement is made to the writers, publishers, and agencies
listed below for permission to reprint material copyrighted or controlled by them.
Please bring to our attention any errors of fact, omission, or copyright.

✈ INTRODUCTION

Henshall, James A. [1881] 1993. "The Philosophy of Angling" from *The Book of Black Bass*. Reprint, Vermont:
    Press of the Sea Turtle.
Dennys, John. [1613] 1993. "The Qualities of an Angler" from *The Secrets of Angling*. Reprint, Vermont: Press of
    the Sea Turtle.

✈ BASS

Bodio, Stephen. 1993. "A Few Words on Bass" from *The Book of Black Bass*. Reprint, Vermont:
    Press of the Sea Turtle.
Seabury, George J. [1890] 1993. "An Ode to Lake Bass" from *The Secrets of Angling*. Reprint, Vermont:
    Press of the Sea Turtle.
McClane, A.J. & Garner, Keith. 1984. "Smallmouth Bass & Largemouth Bass" from *McClane's Gamefish of
    North America*. Reprint, New York: Times Books, a division of Random House, Inc.
Kramer, George. 1990. "Bass & Bassin'" and "Stream & Shore" from *Bass Fishing—An American Tradition*.
    Reprint, San Diego: Thunder Bay.
Grey, Zane. [1908] 1928. "The Lord of Lackawaxen Creek" from *Tales of Fresh-water Fishing*. Reprint, New York:
    Harper Brothers.
Carter, Jimmy. 1994. "Catching Bass on Television" from *An Outdoor Journal*. Reprint: University of Arkansas
    Press.

✈ TROUT

Norman, Geoffrey. 1981. "A Fisherman's Seasons" from *The Ultimate Fishing Book*. Reprint, New York: Houghton
    Mifflin Company.
Smith, Robert H. 1984. "Geology & Trout" from *Native Trout of North America*. Reprint, New York: Frank Amato
    Publications.
Walton, Izaak. [1653] 1993. "Saptogus" from *The Compleat Angler*. Reprint, Vermont: Press of the Sea Turtle.
Wulff, Lee. 1986. "The Trout's World" and "Trout Vision" from *Trout on a Fly*. Reprint, New York: Nick Lyons
    Books.
Traver, Robert. 1964. "Testament of a Fisherman," " On Trout Fishing and the Sturdy Virtues," and "Are All Fisher
    men Alike?" from *Anatomy of a Fisherman*, Reprint, New York: McGraw-Hill.
Traver, Robert. 1984. "The First Day" and "The Last Day," from *Trout Madness*. Reprint, New York: St. Martin's
    Press.
Maclean, Norman. 1976. *A River Runs Through It*. Reprinted by permission of the University of Chicago Press.
Carter, Jimmy. 1994. "Notes of a Fly-fisherman" from *An Outdoor Journal*. Reprinted by permission of the
    University of Arkansas Press.
Russell, R.H. [1902] 1993. "Baptism of the Brook Trout" from *The Speckled Brook Trout*. Reprint, Vermont: Press
    of the Sea Turtle.

✈ CONCLUSION

Haig-Brown, Roderick. 1964. "Ethics & Aesthetics" from *A Primer of Fly-Fishing*. Reprint, Oregon: Douglas &
    McIntyre.
Walton, Izaak. [1653] 1974. "The Angler's Song," from *The Compleat Angler*, 1653. Reprint, Oxford: Oxford
    University Press.

INTRODUCTION

Ode To

BASS & TROUT

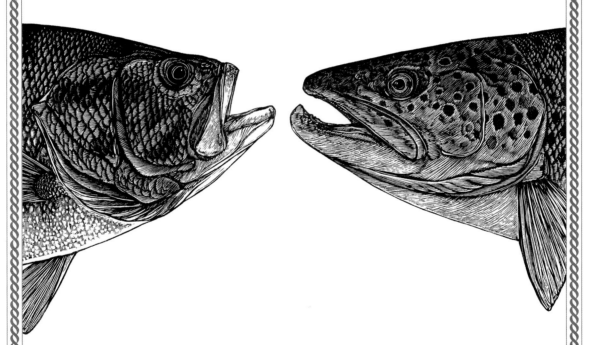

LARGEMOUTH BASS

Micropterus salmoides

BROWN TROUT

Salmo trutta fario

THE PHILOSOPHY

of ANGLING

James A. Henshall
1881

IN THE DAYS of good old Father Izaak Walton, angling was, as stated by him in the title of his famous book, the "contemplative man's recreation." While this is no less true in our own day, the art of angling has extended its sphere of usefulness by becoming not only the recreation of the contemplative man, but of the active, stirring, overworked business and professional man, as well. . . .

Angling is an art, and it is not beneath the dignity of anyone to engage in it as a recreation. It is hallowed by "Meek Walton's heavenly memory," and has been practiced and commended by some of the best and truest and wisest men that ever lived; for, as Father Izaak says: "It is an art, an art worthy of the knowledge and practice of a wise man." Did the art of angling require an apologist, I could here produce evidence, in precept and example, of good and wise men of all ages, from the days of the Fishers of Galilee down to the present time, upholding and commending the moral tendencies and the healthful influ-

ences of the art of angling, and its virtue of making men better physically, intellectually, and spiritually.

"O, sir, doubt not but that angling is an art," says Piscator to Venator, "is it not any art to deceive a Trout with an artificial fly? A Trout is more sharp-sighted than any hawk you have named, and more watchful and timorous than your high-mettled merlin is bold?"

Is it not an art to glide stealthily and softly along the bank of a stream to just where the wary Bass or timid Trout is watching and waiting, ever on the alert for the slightest movement, and keenly alive to each passing shadow; to approach him unawares; to cast the feathery imitation of an insect lightly and naturally upon the surface of the water, without a suspicious splash, and without disclosing to his observant eyes the shadow of the rod or line; to strike the hook into his jaws the instant he unsuspectingly takes the clever ruse into his mouth; to play him, and subdue him, and land him successfully and artistically with a willowy

"DEEP IN THE TURQUOISE POOL"–ADRIANO MANOCCHIA

rod and silken line that would not sustain half his weight out of the water? Is not this any art? Let the doubter try it.

"Doubt not, therefore, sir, but that angling is an art," says Walton, "and an art worth your learning. The question is rather, whether you be capable of learning it?"

Exactly so, Father Izaak; the question is, not merely "to be or not to be," but whether one is "capable" of learning it; for though any one may become a bait-fisher, it is not every one that can learn the fly-fisher's art; for, continues Walton, "he that hopes to be a good angler, must not only bring an inquiring, searching, observing wit, but he must bring a large measure of hope and patience, and a love and propensity to the art itself; but having once got and practiced it, then doubt not but angling will prove to be so pleasant, that it will prove to be, like virtue, a reward to itself."

Excerpted from
THE BOOK OF BLACK BASS

THE QUALITIES
of an ANGLER

John Dennys

1613

But ere I further goe, it shall behove
To shew what gifts and qualities of minde
Belongs to him that doth this pastime love;
And what the vertues are of every kinde
Without the which it were in vaine to prove,
Or to expect the pleasure he should finde,
    No more than he that having store of meate
    Hath lost all lust and appetite to eate.

For what avails to Brooke or Lake to goe,
With handsome Rods and Hookes of divers sort,
Well twisted Lines, and many trinkets moe,
To finde the Fish within their watry fort,
If that the minde be not contented so,
But wants great gifts that should the rest support.
    And make his pleasure to his thoughts agree,
    With these therefore he must endued be.

The first is Faith, not wavering and unstable,
But such as had that holy Patriarch old,
That to the highest was so acceptable
As his increase and of-spring manifolde
Exceeded far the starres innumerable,
So must he still a firme persuasion holde,

That where as waters, brookes, and lakes are found,
There store of Fish without all doubt abound.

For nature that hath made no emptie thing,
But all her workes doth well and wisely frame,
Hath fild each Brooke, each River, Lake and Spring
With creatures, apt to live amidst the same;
Even as the earth, the ayre, and seas doe bring
Forth Beasts, and Birds of sundry sort and name,
    And given them shape, ability, and sence,
    To live and dwell therein without offence.

The second gift and qualitie is Hope,
The anchor-holde of every hard desire;
That having at the day so large a scope,
He shall in time to wished hap aspire,
And ere the Sunne hath left the heav'nly cope,
Obtaine the sport and game he doth desire,
    And that the Fish though sometime slow to bite,
    Will recompence delay with more delight.

The third is Love, and liking to the game,
And to his friend and neighbour dwelling by;
For greedy pleasure not to spoile the same,

Nor of his Fish some portion to deny
To any that are sicklie, weake, or lame,
But rather with his Line and Angle try
   In Pond or Brooke, to doe what in him lyes,
    To take such store for them as may suffice.

Then followeth Patience, that the furious flame
Of Choller cooles, and Passion puts to flight,
As doth a skilfull rider breake and tame,
The Courser wilde, and teach him tread aright:
So patience doth the minde dispose and frame,
To take mishaps in worth, and count them light,
   As losse of Fish, Line, Hooke, or Lead, or all,
    Or other chance that often may befall.

The fift good guift is low Humilitie,
As when a lyon coucheth for his pray

So must he stoope or kneele upon his knee,
To save his line or put the weedes away,
Or lye along sometime if neede there be,
For any let or chance that happen may,
   And not to scorne to take a little paine,
    To serve his turne his pleasure to obtaine.

The sixt is painefull strength and courage good,
The greatest to incounter in the Brooke,
If that he happen in his angry mood,
To snatch your bayte, and beare away your Hooke.
With wary skill to rule him in the Flood
Untill more quiet, tame, and milde he looke,
   And all adventures constantly to beare,
    That may betide without mistrust or feare.

Next unto this is Liberalitie,
Feeding them oft with full and plenteous hand,
Of all the rest a needfull qualitie,
To draw them neere the place where you will stand,
Like to the ancient hospitalitie,
That sometime dwelt in Albions fertile land,
    But now is sent away into exile,
    Beyond the bounds of Issabellas Ile.

The eight is knowledge how to finde the way
To make them bite when they are dull and slow,
And what doth let the same and breedes delay,
And every like impediment to know,
That keepers them from their foode and wanted pray,
Within the streame, or standing waters low,

And with experience skilfully to prove,
    All other faults to mend or to remove.
The ninth is placabilitie of minde,
Contented with a reasonable dish,
Yea though sometimes no sport at all he finde,
Or that the weather prove not to his wish.
The tenth is thankes to that God, of each kinde,
To net and bayt doth send both foule and Fish,
    And still reserve inough in secret store,
    To please the rich, and to relieve the poore.

Th' eleaventh good guift and hardest to indure,
Is fasting long from all superfluous fare,
Unto the which he must himselfe inure,
By exercise and use of dyet spare,
And with the liquor of the waters pure,
Acquaint himselfe if he cannot forbeare,
    And never on his greedy belly thinke,
    From rising sunne untill a low he sincke.

The twelth and last of all is memory,
Remembering well before he setteth out,
Each needfull thing that he must occupy,

And not to stand of any want in doubt,
Or leave something behinde forgetfully:
When he hath walkt the fields and brokes about,
    It were a griefe backe to returne againe,
    For things forgot that should his sport maintaine.

Here then you see what kind of quallities,
An Angler should indued be with all,
Besides his skill and other properties,
To serve his turne, as to his lot doth fall:
But now what season for this exercise,
The fittest is and which doth serve but small,
    My Muse vouchsafe some little ayd to lend,
    To bring this also to the wished end.

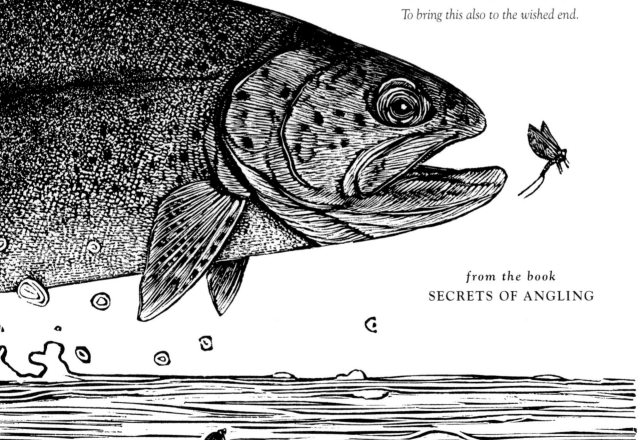

from the book
SECRETS OF ANGLING

"The bass leaped out of a flying splash,

shook himself in a tussle plainly audible,

and slung the hook back at me like a bullet."

—Zane Grey, "The Lord of Lakawaxen Creek"

PART I
BASS

LARGEMOUTH BASS
Micropterus salmoides

"SUMMER REFLECTIONS ON TEN MILE RIVER"—ADRIANO MANOCCHIA

"Because the roots of our more refined fishing are in England,

and England has no real bass, the fish has a problem with image.

This is not a rational matter."

A FEW WORDS

ON BASS

Stephen Bodio
1993

BE HONEST, NOW. Do you pay attention to bass? Not just fish for them when you can't get to your favorite trout stream or lazily, in the dog days of summer, but pay attention to them? Think, even dream about them, as I do?

It is one of the dark unspoken secrets of American sport that, if you do, you are unlikely to be reading essays like this. Although we cherish our traditions of democracy and egalitarianism, other traditions, unspoken and unexamined, run through our ideas of sport like underground rivers, emerging like them in unexpected spots, at inopportune times. Because we do not verbally divide our fish species into "game" and "coarse" the way the English do, we think we are free of social castes and snobbery. We delude ourselves.

I am not talking about rational standards, discrimination, ideas of beauty; all these are things to celebrate. Some fish fight better than others, or taste more delicious; some are more difficult to catch. I, who love catfish, would not compare their muddy colors to the blush of a rainbow trout, the mirror flash of a bonefish, the improbable cloisonné

splendor of a native brookie in spawning season. I'm talking about irrational snobbery here. Greg Keeler once summed it up in two sentences, in his story "Carp of a Parallel Universe": "You're a kid, you're fishing in a river or lake with your Uncle Charlie, and you're delighted because you have finally landed a huge golden-green fish. Just as you lunge for the stringer, Uncle Charlie swears in disgust, picks the fish up by its tail, slams its head against a rock, and heaves it up on the bank to rot." Doesn't that uncomfortable picture say something true about the educated American angler's attitude toward carp, and pickerel, and catfish, and bass?

The particular problem of the bass is that it is considered "common," mundane—not just common as in ordinary but as in vulgar. Because the roots of our more refined fishing are in England, and England has no real bass, the fish has a problem with image. This is not a rational matter. England has no ruffed grouse or bobwhite quail, either, but our class-conscious gunners have adapted their customs and gear to these native birds. Ducks and

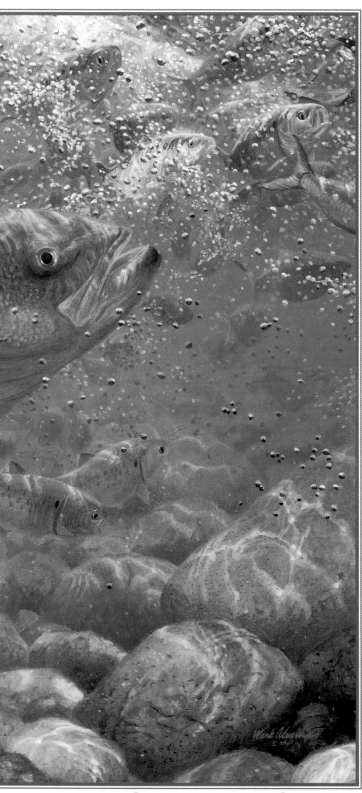

"BREAKING BAD—STRIPED BASS"—MARK SUSINNO

other waterfowl are working man's quarry in Britain, but rich Americans will pay the price of a used car to belong to a duck club. Perhaps the problem is that bass are accessible, to poor men and even children. Upland birds and ducks grow ever more inaccessible even as they, and fine guns, grow more desirable as badges of class. Bass are common currency.

Still worse, as one salmonoid snob once told me, is the matter of bass fanatics. "Not very beautiful people" is how he put it. Well, all right. It's hard for the sporting esthete, never mind the snob (no, they are not necessarily the same person) to summon up anything but a shudder when confronted by rainbow polyester jumpsuits, by candy-apple metal-flake Star-Wars bass boats with boom-box stereo systems and enough paramilitary electronic fish-finding equipment to make Rambo drool, by people who think that "hawg" is a proper term for a hapless eight-pound female fish. But I submit that this is a classic case of blaming the victim. The existence of crass bass tournaments and plastic powerboats does not make the bass a crass plastic fish.

Bass are common, as in ubiquitous. They are also subtle in their color and shape. So are ruffed grouse. Catfish (and woodcock) at least stand out from the crowd in their eccentric grotesquerie. Trout, and ducks, and pheasants, are bold and graceful in their shapes and colors. Any calendar artist can make something pretty of a rainbow or a mallard; it takes a real artist to show the inherent beauty of the dead-leaf designs on a grouse, the distilled essence of subaqueous light, pond weed patterns, of power and speed held in reserve, that go to make up a bass or pickerel. No wonder that most pictures of bass are simple snapshots of mouth, open, surrounded by splash. It's easy. I'm not sure that bass has yet found its portraitist. What could the Dürer of the hare portrait do with our solid subtle citizen of a fish?

Bass lures suffer by comparison to trout flies, too. In the Nineteenth, a more leisurely century, bass flies resembled larger and more fanciful versions of brook trout attractors, big gaudy concoctions of married duck wing, with striped chenille bodies of black and gold. They apparently worked. Even then you could find goggle-eyed lures with gaping mouths. Although these were meant to resemble frogs and baitfish, how many swimming frogs do you see with open mouths? They look more like those magazine-cover leaping bass in minia-ture, with the addition of wiggly legs and marabou feathers. We make our lures fit our fish, or our images of them.

After World War Two new technologies abandoned aesthetics entirely. Now we have purple jelly-worms, Christmas trees of metal, dayglo salamanders, and worse. People who scorned flies as effete and who apparently were squeamish about real organic bait went around flinging the hardware store at the poor bass, further lowering its image. Again, it's not the bass's fault. You could probably catch more trout on such things, too, but nobody wants to.

Easy? Well, any bass is a lot simpler than a trout sipping midge pupae in a level chalk-stream. But then, so are most trout. Many chil-dren first learn to fish by catching spawning bass. The pale circles that the earnestly parental bass clear in pond shallows (trout, of course, do not care for their young) are one of the first things that any beginner can learn to see through the surface, the neophyte's earliest

primer in "reading the water." The satisfactory thump of the defensive strike when anything invades the nursery is a real and tangible reward to kids, who need success. And, finally, to any sensitive child, the discomfort and guilt that comes from the realization that you are killing a parent for protecting its young might well be the first lesson in responsibility, and therefore stewardship and fairness and the idea of "sport," that he or she gets.

I guess my idea is that we should look at the fish itself, not the man-made trappings. I don't mean to repeat Henshall's famous words, which I've been trying to avoid so far—you know, "pound for pound and inch for inch, the gamest fish that swims." It's true, but only par-tially, and he was talking about the slightly more socially acceptable of the two bass, the small-mouth (it's skinnier and lives in rivers) and, well, so what? What I want you to do is to con-sider your experience with bass, and remember.

My own love of bass comes from such memories, some thirty-odd years past, some as recent as yesterday. Although I fished for bass all my life I came to a real appreciation of them here in New Mexico. I discovered "bass" as a worthy object for reflection post-catfish, never mind post-trout. It was an almost spiritual rev-elation, a "literary" one if you will: bass, more than any other fish, are the animals that make connections between all my disparate sporting lives, between childhood and present, east and west, still waters and moving, winning and loss, past and present, life and death.

Childhood: the first thing that I am con-scious of killing was a big largemouth, one of those spawners on a nest. I know I caught a fish—sunnies, pickerel, even a few native

brook trout—before that, in the company of my father. But on that day I had taken my bicycle to Ames Long Pond, on the Ames estate in Easton, Massachusetts, to fish (the first time?) on my own. For a while I contented myself with flipping worm fragments into the lily pads. Each cast caught a miniature bluegill, which I dumped into a plastic bucket full of water. But then I saw a big shadow with a dark line on its side hovering beside a patch of sand the size of a trashcan lid, about ten feet from the bank.

I knew this was a bass. Bass ate crayfish, not worms. (I didn't know then that she would have probably hit a bare hook tossed into that sacred circle.) I climbed down into the dark tunnel under the road that took the overflow from the pond and began to turn over rocks. In a few minutes I came up with a dark, pinching, kicking little lobster, a miniature monster out of those bad science fiction movies popular then, and hooked it firmly under its carapace. It was a little scary dealing with its alien life and clanking defiance. I returned to the bank and lobbed it into the strike zone.

She hit instantly. Of course time has magnified her fight, but she was the first thing that ever put a deep bend in my rod. I remember thinking that this, at last, was fishing. But my cheap spinning tackle held together (of course—but I remember my fear that it wouldn't, that nothing so slender could resist such a pull) until I skidded her, quivering and flapping and so alive, onto the sandy bank.

My first emotion was pride: now my parents would know that I could CATCH FISH. My second was fear: what should I do with her?

She wouldn't easily fit in the bucket, and she was jumping two feet—so I remember—into the air. I dragged her further from the edge and waited for her to die.

She didn't. After what seemed like hours but was probably about ten minutes, I recalled my father's snapping the neck of a big pickerel the previous fall. I attempted to bend her head around, but my hands slipped on her slime. I retreated, and waited some more.

At last she seemed still. I threaded her on a stick, through her gills, and, to my horror, she began to flop around again. In tears, I removed the stick and carried her to the water, where I placed her upright in the shallows. She sunk to the bottom. I righted her, and she sunk again.

22

Finally, I took her out and put her in the bucket where she lay on her side, at peace. Now she was dull, no longer shining. I stared at her a long time, then hooked the bucket onto the handlebars and pedaled home. I was not exactly in despair, but I was thoughtful. My parents did make proud noises when we cooked her that evening, but her taste is not part of my memory.

East and west, past and present, life and death. When I discovered fly-fishing, as a young man, I didn't live near any trout streams. I learned how to catch a bunch of deer hair in a loop of thread so that, when I tugged it down around a hook clamped in a vise, the hair flared in a corona, a wild mane, that could clip into any shape I wished. I built floating frogs which I tossed on short level leaders into the darkness under flame-like cedars in certain boggy ponds close to home, still in Massachusetts. I would let them float in stillness and silence, then move my rod with just a tremor, almost a heartbeat. If I did it right the furry frog would disappear in a splash that sounded as though I had clapped a bucket down on the black surface. Then, if I could steer clear of the weeds, I might see that animate mouth standing on its tail next to my canoe, just like on the covers of all those magazines. In those days I was very poor, and I didn't let many go.

Still later, in Maine, with my late partner Betsy, I discovered the joys of river small-mouths in the Saco. We'd take out a canoe, thread minnows or salmon streamers with trailing hooks on fly rods, and troll them behind the boat. These weren't big fish; a couple of pounds was the average. But the first one pulled the rod from Betsy's inexperienced hands; luckily, I caught it before it was gone, and returned it to her. In a life of improbable travel and adventure she had done almost no fishing, and that little was handed to her as apart of other experiences. "Did you ever catch a fish? I had asked. "Oh, once . . . a roosterfish, in the Sea of Cortez." (We had read our Steinbeck.) "It was exciting, but ugly." Now she fought it like a little girl, giggling, and adamantly refused to release it. I remember eating that one.

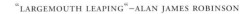

"LARGEMOUTH LEAPING"–ALAN JAMES ROBINSON

And west . . . after her death, searching for something to do in a life gone gray and meaningless. I returned to the alien salt-cedar jungles along the Rio Grande where we had spent long idle warm nights fishing for monster catfish by the light of Coleman lanterns. I had been in the east for eight months, but even the Saco smallmouths had failed to excite me without my partner. Now I heard a babble of blackbirds and a thrum of frogs across the river, where the railroad bridge crossed and ran along the foot of a black volcanic mesa. We had never crossed, but I remembered that there was supposed to be a pond, an old oxbow, there.

I crossed over the dangerous water with the carelessness that comes from a long period of pain, never looking down. Hidden beyond the feathery tamarisk fringe, the pond looked like nothing I had ever seen. But the lily pads and cattails seemed familiar, and when I rolled the deer-hair frog from the bank—no room for a back cast here—the strike brought me back, not to the Saco, but the black water of Ponkapoag Pond.

It's fall now, and I believe I'll drive down to the Big River and cross that bridge. In the fall everything is on the move. There will be ducks, and shorebirds from the Arctic, and perhaps a flock of migrating white pelicans riding the thermals over the mesa like improbably beautiful pterodactyls. Warblers and swallows will be dipping flies from the surface, and the bass will be swirling under the rings they make like some impossibly overpopulated diorama of predation in a museum—but alive, alive and moving. I will fish in the present, and think about the past, and muse about the people and places that bass have brought to me. These are my connections, and I owe them to bass, those common fish I can find everywhere. And I bet you can do the same, wherever and whoever you are.

Excerpted from
A FEW WORDS ON BASS

AN ODE
to LAKE BASS

George J. Seabury

1890

Canto I. To The Oswego or Large Mouth Bass

Walton's slaves, with all your might
Bend to your oars, the ground's in sight,
Feeding bass the surface break,
Rollicking o'er the placid lake.

'Mid rocks and stumps, now on their ground,
Our dipping oars the only sound,
Above their haunts we smoothly glide,
And noiseless cast from side to side,
Lashing the line in graceful curves,
When lo! The touch that thrills the nerves
Excites the pulse, and lends suspense
To sport that gladdens every sense!

Responsive to the nerves' appeal,
Instinctively we turn the reel
The line is strained, the tip is crooked,
A brave Oswego, firmly hooked.

Comes slowly in, each inch resisting,
Plunging, swirling, jerking, twisting;
Now in the air, now fiercely diving,

Then madly for the Lake's depths striving;
Seeking in some romantic nook,
To free him from the cruel hook,
'Round obstacles he wildly shoots,
'Neath weeds, logs, brush and snarly roots.
But naught avails, he's hooked too well.
The reel's sharp click shall sound his knell
As quickly the line to our view brings the captive,
With desp'rate resistance contesting his fate;
The lust of the sportsman by victory excited
Surpasses the Oswego's greed for its bait.

Alas, poor creature! Though losing they freedom,
Because in they strength thou would'st prey on the weak,
So bold, yet so helpless, we grieve at thy struggles,
That man, in such cruelty pastime should seek.

Above thee the waves are singing sad dirges;
Thy doom is foretold in each brief lasting note,
Thou lashest the surface again but in fury,
One whirl of the rod–thou art safe in the boat!
From side to side rebounding,

Rising, drumming, jumping, pounding,
Rolling, gasping, weakening fast,
Struggling to the very last.

When exhaustion and despair
Blend in mute appealing prayer,
With a tremor and a sigh
You fix your red-fringed eye.
Then in death you quiet lie.

Brave Oswego! No waters hold
Marauding cannibal more bold
Than thou, who knew no fear,
Merc'less hunger has brought thee here,
The prey of man, who lies in wait,
To lure thee with a phantom bait.

Canto II. To The Small Mouth Bass

To the lake again we consign our line,
The casting rod for the troll resign;
At dreamer's pace, along we float,
Light ripples splashing 'gainst our boat;
When, like a flash, the signal's felt,
That tells of savage strike just dealt
The shining bait far out of sight:

Jupiter! What a vicious bite.
See! Up he leaps with lightning speed,
The prisoner struggling to be freed
From torturing hook he can't displace;
Now high he's jumping into space,
Shaking in mid-air, his ruby gills,
Threshing the water into bubbling rills.

Vaulting again, with clownish mien,
Then plunging back, no more is seen:
Punter, be wary! The line is caught,
Row slow, a battle's to be fought!

How gallantly he comes along,
Pulls like a sailor long and strong.
Give him no particle of slack;
Hold steady, though the line crack.
The tension now is far too great,
For 'tis a bass of mighty weight.

Cautiously we reel him in,
On the surface 'pears a fin,
Now on his nose he takes a spin,
For freedom fights with all his might,
Now in the air, now lost to sight.

Swirling, charging, then retreating,
Perhaps our fondest aims defeating,
Under the boat now deeply diving,
For liberty still bravely striving;
Then glistens in resplendent light
A five-pound Black—enchanting sight!
Row fast! Into deep waters settle;
He forges ahead with martial mettle.

'Mong rocks and brush, away he goes,
Writhing in agonizing throes.

Aha! He weakens; Punter! Steady!
Be for every movement ready.
Bravo! The work is coolly done;
Keen is the artful angler's fun.

Beneath him plunge the landing net
On victory now all eyes are set,
With trembling limbs and mind excited,
Our fondest hopes are quickly blighted

Spellbound! A yell! A faulty snell!
The bass breaks from the angler's cell,
Splashing, dashing, away he goes,
Mocking the angler's frantic woes.

Chagrined by defeat, the passions inflamed,
Each for the loss by the other is blamed;
Thus anglers merry, who rudeness disdain
Now rave in their fury like fish in seine.

Right here, dear friends, let us re-bait our line.
To narrate the sequel, excuse, truly thine.

Excerpted from
AN ODE TO LAKE BASS

"RIGHT ON THE MONEY"—ADRIANO MANOCCHIA

"But it's that magic pool shadowed by moss-and-lichen-covered ledges that brings me back, year after year, where I once lost a big smallmouth bass that made three gill-flaring jumps before vanishing in its depths."

SMALLMOUTH BASS

& LARGEMOUTH BASS

A. J. McClane & Keith Gardner
1984

Smallmouth Bass

To me, autumn is a wonderful time of the year to be on a bass river. The mountains are aflame with color and the air is clear. A kingfisher will study my pool down the arrow of his beak, then *scree* in swift departure. I can hear grosbeaks and thrushes rustling among fallen leaves while whistling chipmunks gaily gather beechnuts for a winter's feast. Woodcock will be migrating down the valley and geese are trading cornfields across a cobalt sky, their raucous honking applauded by the laughter of the river's currents. But it's that magic pool shadowed by moss- and lichen-covered ledges that brings me back, year after year, where I once lost a big smallmouth bass that made three gill-flaring jumps before vanishing in its depths. I want to believe the same fish is still in its crepuscular lair waiting for my fly, but this brief encounter occurred a decade ago, and to materialize again, it would have to be over a hundred years old by human chronology. However, game fish are as compelling as the country they keep, and the rod-throbbing

apparition of a bronzeback leaping over and shattering a mirrored surface turned scarlet and gold by maple and oak makes such sentimental hopes inevitable. Even a roll call of smallmouth rivers stirs up ghosts of seasons past—the Shenandoah, James, Potomac, Susquehanna, St. Lawrence, the Snake—indeed, the bronzeback haunts far more waters today than in the seventeenth century when Quebec's French settlers knew him by the Algonquin Indian name *achigan*, or "ferocious."

The original distribution of smallmouth bass in North America extended from northern Minnesota to Quebec and down to the Allegheny Mountains, south to northern Alabama and eastern Oklahoma. This range has been greatly increased in Canada and the United States in areas adjacent to its native habitats and in widely dispersed watersheds elsewhere, being absent from Alaska, Louisiana and Florida. It is found in seven Canadian Provinces but the only notable fisheries occur in Ontario, Quebec and New Brunswick. In the nineteenth century, the smallmouth was considered a superior game fish to the largemouth bass, and transplants began in 1850 with a token twenty-seven fish delivered from Saratoga Lake, New York, to East Wareham, Massachusetts. Four years later, the by now legendary General William Shriver railroaded just twelve bass, a literal drop in a bucket which was hung on a locomotive water tender, from West Virginia to the Chesapeake and Ohio Canal. The canal drained into the Potomac River where they proliferated and became the seed for many subsequent plantings. By the 1880s, the smallmouth was widely distributed in the eastern half of the United States and the popularity of bass fishing exploded.

The controversy over which species is the gamest, the largemouth or the smallmouth, continued into the twentieth century with such exponents of the latter as author Zane Grey, who lived at Lackawaxen on the Delaware River. In an article published by *Field & Stream* in May 1912, he enigmatically challenged (after describing the capture of forty bass in one day, not one under 3 pounds and some over 4) his peers.

I have caught a good many Delaware bass running over six pounds and I want to say that these long, black and bronze fellows, peculiar to the swift water of this river, are the most beautiful and gamy fish that swim. I never get tired of studying them and catching them. It took years to learn how to catch them. Perhaps some day I shall tell you how to do it. But not until I have had the pleasure of seeing Dilg and Davis, and other celebrated fishermen who have not yet honored me with a visit, breaking their arms and hearts trying to induce one of these grand fish to an artificial fly. Because, gentlemen, they will not do it.

Delaware smallmouths were, of course, being caught on plugs, spinners, spoons and flies but Grey, a confirmed live-bait fisherman at the time, may well have scored heavily, although the weights he gave (none under 3 pounds) boggle the imagination for river bass, even in a pristine environment.

The smallmouth is a large member of the sunfish family (*Centrarchidae*) in a genus popularly known as the black basses. However, adult black bass are not black. Newly hatched fry are nearly transparent but after the yolk sac is absorbed and the tiny fish are free swimming, they gradually turn black, hence the name. At a length of about a half inch, they become dark green, and with age the smallmouth turns to a patinaed bronze, which inspired the *nom de guerre* "bronzeback." Black bass have suffered many scientific names since that French naturalist Lacépède first described both the smallmouth and largemouth in 1802. The single specimen of the smallmouth that he studied had a deformed dorsal, so the generic Latin, *Micropterus* (which means "small fin"), is misleading. Yet the name was finally adopted based on historic precedence for all six black bass species.

The smallmouth bass encompasses two subspecies: the northern smallmouth *Micropterus dolomieui dolomieui* and the Neosho smallmouth, *Micropterus d. velox*. The Neosho smallmouth is found in the Neosho River and tributaries of the Arkansas River in Oklahoma, Arkansas and Missouri. The original habitat of this subspecies has been greatly reduced due to the construction of impoundments and subsequent environmental changes. The name *velox* means "swift" in reference to its characteristic as a game fish. The Neosho is more slender than the northern form and differs in that its lower jaw projects beyond the snout, and the upper mandible extends to, or nearly below, the posterior margin of the eye, as opposed to the anterior in the more common smallmouth.

THE CYCLE OF THE SEASON

In spring, smallmouth bass begin coming inshore when the water temperature reaches 55°F, and begin spawning as it approaches 60°F, which occurs from late April to early July, depending on latitude. The male bass constructs a circular nest on a gravel substrate in the shallows of a lake or stream by sweeping silt and debris from the bottom. These spawning areas are usually at depths of 2 to 10 feet on a gently sloping shore free of wave action (or away from strong currents in a stream). The female bass comes coyly from deep water where the male repetitively chases her to the nest before pairing is accomplished. Eggs and milt are emitted at brief intervals of seconds in duration until the act is completed and the female departs. The male guards the eggs and subsequently may spawn with other females using the same nest, defensively remaining at the site to discourage predators until the schooled black fry are free swimming—usually a period of about one month. Nesting smallmouths are especially vulnerable to angling; however, because of a high reproductive potential there is no closed season in many states. Also, catch-and-release fishing is very popular in most camps today. In large bodies of water with minimal fishing pressure, smallmouth bass populations thrive with no apparent decline in the quality of the sport.

During the summer months, smallmouths abandon the lake shoreline and retreat to depths of 15 to 30 feet. This varies regionally and with prevailing weather conditions. The bass feed most actively in a water temperature range of 60° to 70°F, avoiding areas that exceed 73°F. However, they are often found for brief periods on mid-lake reefs and shoals at depths of 2 to 5 feet in the heat of August and will frequently return to forage along the shoreline during morning and evening hours. Extensive mayfly hatches or an abundance of wind-borne, terrestrial insects will also cause the fish to feed in warm surface water. But cooling temperatures in autumn bring smallmouths back into the shallows, which can be a peak time for trophy fish that fatten like black bears before hibernation. With the approach of winter, northern smallmouths move into deeper water. This school migration begins when water temperatures start to drop in the late fall, literally a mass exodus at 50°F, and the fish settle in currentless places devoid of light, squeezing between rock crevices, or settling in deep holes and even submerged logs. The bass become dormant as temperatures reach the lower 40s. Angling is, of course, possible in warmer southern waters, although the bass may be less active during severe or prolonged cold spells. However, some of the heaviest smallmouths ever taken nationally in recent years, fish from 8 pounds, 4 ounces to 9 pounds, 3 ounces, were caught during the November to February period in Alabama and Tennessee while northern bass were comatose.

FLY-FISHING
FOR SMALLMOUTHS

In rivers and lake shallows, the smallmouth bass is a classic quarry of the fly-fisherman during the spring and fall seasons. Summer fishing is less reliable when the bronzebacks usually retreat to deep water. The smallmouth can be taken on dry flies, wet flies, nymphs, streamers and, of course, bass bugs. Back in the days when James A. Henshall was codifying the tribal lore of black bass (*Book of the Black Bass*, Robert Clarke & Co., Cincinnati, 1881), he favored a split-bamboo rod weighing 8 ounces of not more than 11 feet in length. Add to this the hard rubber, German silver, or brass "click reel" popular in that era, which weighed from 10 to 12 ounces, and the angler was painfully swinging 1 to 1 1/4 pounds in repetitive casts. Since Henshall's observations were often sparsely purposive, his reference to the "general demoralization and used up condition of the flexors and extensors of my arms" was perhaps less a tribute to the sporting qualities of black bass, than the gameness of the angler.

Modern day bass fly rods and reels are, of course, much lighter; however, some distinction can be made between an all-purpose outfit capable of bucking winds that blow off the Beaufort scale (a condition common when fishing for Lake Okeechobee largemouths) while casting No. 1/0 and 2/0 plastic bugs, and smallmouth requirements. For bass fishing in general, a composite graphite/fiberglass or boron rod in an 8 1/2-to 9-foot length, weighing 2 7/8 to 3 1/8 ounces, together with a large single action reel of aluminum or magnesium allow of, say, 3 1/2 ounces has a total weight of 6 1/2 or 7 ounces. Such tackle is a sheer joy to cast with and has the backbone to throw large wind-resistant lures with an 8-weight forward line. However, the smallmouth specialist can use shorter and lighter rods, especially for river bass where lures on No. 4 to 10 hooks are generally more effective. I prefer a 1 7/8-ounce, 8-foot graphite rod calibered for a 6-weight line in a double taper.

→ Largemouth Bass

No species of game fish has been more inspirational in swelling the ranks of North American anglers than the largemouth bass. In 1968, an Alabama insurance salesman named Ray Scott decided that the world, or the United States, or at least the Deep South, needed a professional bass fishing tournament circuit modeled on professional tennis and golf. As its Pied Piper, his Bass Anglers Sportsmen Society (B.A.S.S.), now boasting a membership of 400,000, was so successful that it instigated countless imitators until today hundreds of bass lakes host competitive fishing events. Organized on a catch-and-release basis, with points for returning live fish, they have brought technical advances in boat design, tackle design, and outdoor clothing design, and enormous publicity for the no-kill concept. In addition, they have created a cabalistic language that only another bass fisherman can comprehend. Over the years, these tournaments have developed into big-money events with heavy press and television coverage. Prior to B.A.S.S., fishing contests in the United States had been largely limited to local chamber of commerce promotional affairs, while American anglers marveled that European, and especially British and French, fishermen were so intensely organized for "match" fishing. Now everything has changed and the American national gift for excess has spawned an entirely new profession—the bass tournament angler. The competition is keen, and the top moneymakers are formidable fishermen who follow the circuit the year-round. Of course, the smallmouth bass is encompassed in tournaments, but the largemouth, with its greater geographical distribution, is the principal quarry. While there are those in the parish who frown on placing a price on Walton's gentle art, the game is firmly established in our national angling scene.

Largemouth bass are the giants of the *Centrarchidae* or sunfishes. This family is native only to North America and consists of thirty species, the smallest of which, the Everglades pygmy sunfish (*Elassoma evergladei*), becomes a trophy at 1 $\frac{1}{2}$ inches. The largemouth becomes a trophy at whatever size you deem it so, but any weight that would exceed the 22-pound, 4-ounce world record established in 1932 is the ultimate goal of serious bass anglers. Of the six black basses, the largemouth is unique by a jaw that extends past its eye, and a

complete separation of the first and second dorsal fins. The name bass is from the Old English *baers*, meaning bristly, and that first dorsal can puncture your hand if the fish is grasped across the back, though experienced anglers are seldom wounded; the almost toothless mouth is fringed with brush-like cardiform teeth reminiscent of coarse sandpaper, and the fish can be grasped by its lower jaw. A "lipped" bass will become almost inert when lifted from the water.

These slab-sided, lacustrine fish with broad homocercal tails and extensive fin area have evolved for agility rather than speed, so angling for them is for the most part a leisurely sport. It lacks both the brute test of stamina that successful offshore saltwater fishing becomes and the arm-flailing, against-the-current physicality of stream trout fly-fishing. (It is in fact perverse to fish for largemouth bass in running water because they avoid it and will invariably locate the stillest water to be found. You can selectively fish for them in a mixed population of river fish by seeking the bottom of the deepest pools, flotsam-bearing eddies or adjacent sloughs.)

Nevertheless, an agile predator that can grow to more than 20 pounds (in very few environments, which we will discuss later) is bound to be a popular quarry, because the necessary suddenness of its attacks will often make your gooseflesh prickle. A smallmouth bass can make a surface lure fall into a mute, momentary hole in the lake, and a trout will take an insect with the tiniest of dimples, but largemouth habitually kill at the top with vigor. The thrust of their feeding seems to be that anything on the surface is edible and might escape. Underwater they just inhale; evolution does not design maws of such prodigious dimensions whimsically. However, they do have preferred food forms, as some fisheries biologists learned to their sorrow.

For decades the United States government, acting through the Hatchery Division of the Fish and Wildlife Service of the Department of the Interior, and the Soil Conservation Service of the Department of Agriculture, would subsidize a farmer who wanted to bulldoze a stock pond. Most state fish and game departments also contributed their advice or hatchery product. Everyone was certain that millions of ponds full of fish would be A Good Thing. And there was universal agreement that the warm-water pond fishery should be predicated on the piscine world's most inseparable predator-prey relationship: largemouth bass and bluegill sunfish. Millions of ponds now glitter across the face of North America as you overfly. Just manufacturing the bulldozers kept an army of plebs employed, but the sport proved disappointing.

Biologists have since learned that though largemouth will, of course, eat bluegills, they would prefer not to. Being kin, the bluegill is bristly, too, and bass much prefer prey with soft-rayed fins. Shiners and minnows are lovely, and in two-tiered impoundments with warm shallows for bass and cool depths for trout, the bass will forage out of their temperature preferendum to gulp down trout with alacrity. Indeed, in certain southern California impoundments, where the Florida-strain largemouth reproduces naturally and

plants of hatchery rainbows are regularly made to sustain a put-and-take trout fishery, largemouth bass consider the familiar rumble of an approaching hatchery truck to be tantamount to a farmhouse dinner gong.

It was also reported that in a bass-bluegill pond, the availability of bass to angling, combined with the reproductive efficiency of bluegills, soon reduced the bass population and allowed an enormous overpopulation of stunted bluegills. A superabundance of small bluegills will predate on both species, as both ova and juveniles, to the extent that reproduction is virtually prohibited. The afflicted farm ponds then achieved the next stage of degradation and became a biomass of thumb-sized bluegills and a few elderly bass who had only to inhale to be satiated.

Sadder and wiser, as the era of great impoundments began—the sort of superfluminae that would attract urban masses who lacked access to farm ponds—the fisheries scientist found a new prey hero: gizzard shad (*Dorosoma cepedianum*). This slab-sided herring is ubiquitous in eastern North America from Minnesota to Mexico. Rather than filter-feeding plankton as the other shads do, it grubs plant detritus out of the bottom mud, and grows spectacularly, which is a flaw from the viewpoint of largemouth. They must catch a gizzard shad young before it becomes too large to swallow (they top off at 3 pounds and 18 inches). Big bass love big gizzard shad, but few bass become *that* big. The fisheries biologists are now putting their trust in striped bass to crop the gizzard shad resource.

Two fish make perfect largemouth fodder: Another herring, the thread fin shad (*D. petenense*), seldom grows larger than 8 inches, has

"OPPORTUNITY KNOCKS"–MARK SUSINNO

soft fins and is eminently acceptable to large-mouth. It has been widely stocked in bass impoundments, as has been the golden shiner (*Notemigonus crysoleucas*), a minnow that is enjoying a nationwide population explosion because it is a hardy baitfish and because its breeding season is very long, so for most of the year minnowettes are available to tiny bass,

minnows to ordinary bass and 7-to 10-inchers to big bass. These two forage fishes have been the inspiration of many plastic-tailed jigs, countless commercial plugs and a few streamer fly patterns.

Crayfish and shrimp are preferred foods of largemouth. The fish must have cast-iron stomachs because they will gulp down hard-shelled, fully clawed adult specimens with gusto. Crayfish are largely nocturnal, but when you see an individual occupying shallow water in daylight there is usually an explanation for such atypical behavior: It has just endured the fright of its life. With a clipped-deer-hair crayfish fly on a sinking line and short leader, cast to where the crayfish is *looking*.

The undershot jaw and quasi-dorsally mounted eyes of a largemouth bass mean they have evolved for feeding upward. This makes them outstanding candidates for surface lures, a fact obscured for years by the popularity of plastic worms and jigs. These bottom-crawling artificials are unquestionably effective, but millions of insects, ducklings, voles and other surface-swimming creatures go down the gullets of bass, and anglers who do not habitually fish on top of the water are simply sacrificing sport.

In a subjective sense, there are three largemouth bass: a northern strain of late spring spawners, a Florida strain that probably spawns year-round but with a peak in February and March, and hybrids of the two. The latter occur both naturally and of recent years in hatcheries. The IGFA all-tackle world record of 22 pounds, 4 ounces was set in 1932 at Montgomery Lake, Georgia, and was almost certainly a natural intergrade. The outstanding underwater filmmaker Glen Lau, diving in Lake Miramar in southern California, saw a female largemouth that he estimated at 28 pounds. Lau's experience is such that he would be only ounces off scale weight. This fish would be either a stocked Florida strain or a natural hybrid. Florida largemouth differ morphologically from the northerns only in an elevated scale count,

which makes excellent sense—their scales must encompass more bass than do those of northern fish.

Largemouth black bass spawn by nesting in shallow water beds formed by the little males fanning an area 1 or 2 feet in diameter with their tails to rid it of detritus. The males are a quite pugnacious fish all the time, but even more vigorously so when building and protecting their nest. The principal enemy of a brood once it is spawned will be bluegill sunfish, who are adept at making egg-stealing forays at lightning speed. A bedding male is not one to take lightly the invasion of his bed, and a streamer fly or popping bug is famously effective both before and after the spawn.

Our ancestors favored bass flies made with waterfowl breast feathers as wings, which when boldly dyed can have both the shape and colors of sunfish. The current fashion is for streamer flies. It should be borne in mind that our ancestors were country folk and we are not. Their opportunities for fish watching were in multiples of ours, but they had no biologists studying bass and making mass experiments in predator-prey relationships. We now know that slender, soft-rayed prey is the largemouth's preference and our flies and plugs reflect that progress. Fat lures still work well on bass conditioned to avoid thin ones. Many fish learn rapidly.

For his nesting site, the male bass prefers to put his back up against some sort of wall to keep his brood under his gaze and force danger to approach from ahead. He also wants water that is, and will remain, clean because if litter gets in with his brood, fanning to remove it may disturb the eggs. I was making a television film in southern Florida on a lake bearing a large population of the scoters universally called coots. The birds were feeding in their usual fashion by diving for bottom weed and surfacing to gulp what they had uprooted. They are not tidy feeders and a steady northeast wind had spread uneaten fragments over the lake. We had to fish plastic worms rigged in the weedless Texas style to avoid constant fouling, but had difficulty locating the beds until Virgil Ward reasoned that the only proper locale for nests was upwind of the coots, where a few yards of calm water were protected from the wind by a wall of emergent vegetation. He was right. The beds were typically Florida calcareous soil, startlingly white against the surrounding dark bottom. We caught an enormous number of bass up to 10 pounds, a good weight even for the Florida strain. Other good walls for male bass to nest against are cypress, drowned timber, boulders and even just a close scattering of large rocks.

For a few days before spawning, the little males school in groups and the big females in their own aggregations. If trophy hunting, and you catch a 1- or 2-pound fish, it is probably best to move on. Females have been observed thumping their flanks against logs, undoubtedly to loosen the eggs. The invitation to spawn comes when the male leaves his nest, swims up to a bass and begins nipping about its head. Since it is characteristic of all (or most) animals that the sexes have a distinctive bouquet, he has probably already determined her female nature, but they may be able to sex each other visually by size because males will sometimes swim a number of yards directly to a female. On the bed together the spawning can take hours in cool water, only minutes when it warms up.

Bedding bass have always been fished and the consensus of contemporary fisheries biologists is that even catch-and-release impairs the spawning success by weakening the breeding couple and destroying their resolve to defend the eggs until they hatch. However, many biologists also doubt the efficacy of hook-and-line to seriously affect a population larger than a farm pond. Even in a heavily fished pond the fish populations may have been skewed by angling, but the biomass remains essentially the same. Where human beings have frequently made deep incursions into bass populations, the means have been deterioration of water quality through pollution and habitat destruction. In largemouth bass waters, there is an enormous overproduction of eggs. They were intended from the beginning to feed bluegills and glass minnows. Of course, commercial fishing with seine and gillnets, with limbline, trotline, snatch hooks, grab hooks, slat basket, jug, spearing and other ingenious engines has been used at various times to reduce largemouth populations, but commercial traffic in the black basses became illegal thanks to the efforts of United States Senator Harry B. Hawes (Dem., Missouri), whose book *My Friend the Black Bass* (New York, Stokes, 1930) reported his successful leadership of that particular conservation movement.

Most bass caught are small males. One radio-tagging experiment with sixteen tagged male bass reported fourteen of them succumbed to angling in a single spawning season. That sort of fish can be amusing on light fly or spinning tackle, but most anglers are equipped

(and intent) on catching the big females, and here we get into theories of where and how to fish for largemouth that I believe are ultimately dependent on the sex of the fish. The big bass seem to be much more given to deep-water suspension, and that implies segregation by sexes. They also hunt in the warm shallows during summer nights, which we will discuss shortly.

Since largemouth can tolerate a wide variety of environmental conditions, they have been made ubiquitous throughout the United States, save for Alaska. It has been estimated that nearly half of all American anglers are primarily bass fishermen, which reflects not their superiority as a sporting quarry over, say, Atlantic salmon, but their overwhelming availability. It is only of recent years that a few fisheries biologists have entertained the concept that the enormous population of black basses might be subject to overharvest. Human population growth and future reductions in the workweek may bring widespread overharvest within credibility. An A. C. Nielsen survey of 1982 reported 14 percent of the U.S. population were bass fishermen. That would at the time total about 31,000,000 people, a very large number to ask any recreational resource to support.

If the present generous bag and possession regulations of most states are ultimately, under excessive angling pressure, to turn into catch-and-release, bass fishermen will learn there are better fish to fry.

Almost every one of the contiguous states is currently managing one or more bass lakes under special bag or length regulations to evaluate the effects of angling pressure. Within a decade or so there should be a data base from these experiments. In Texas, they estimate that large "bass" impoundments have a non-bass fin fish component of 95 percent or more, but the popularity of bass fishing is crucial to the tourism industry. Confronted with such a dilemma, everyone from investment bankers to gallus-snapping guides suddenly becomes a born-again conservationist.

The only states that have yielded largemouth bass of 15 pounds or more are California, Florida, Georgia and South Carolina. Glen Lau's 28-pounder may not represent the ultimate size attainable in a lightly harvested climax population of Florida. In 1773, the Pennsylvania naturalist William Bartram embarked on a four-year exploration of the American Southeast that took him far up the north-flowing St. Johns River in Florida. A party of traders he was traveling with showed him how they fished for "trout" with a lure made from the tail hair of a whitetail deer and some shreds from a red garter tied on three stout hooks, the famous "bob" or "jiggerbob" they had learned from the Indians they traded with. Bartram reported:

> *The unfortunate cheated trout instantly springs from under the weeds and seizes the supposed prey. They frequently weigh fifteen, twenty, and thirty pounds, and are delicious food.*

He is welcome to them as table fare, but I have never hooked a largemouth that would not jump at least once, and the prospect of a 30-pounder sailing through the air is awesome. Bartram ate his broiled bass slathered with a sauce of oil, oranges and salt and pepper, which no doubt contributed greatly to their palatability.

The biggest Florida-strain fish of recent years have been coming out of the impoundments maintained by San Diego's Water Utilities Department. These reservoirs were stocked with Florida largemouth in the late 1950s and by 1973 had produced a state record just 1 ounce shy of 21 pounds. A national craze for Florida broodstock developed and in many states the gene pool of well-adapted local strains is endangered by plantings of Florida fish, some of them made by fish and game departments that should be more concerned with the resource and less with the tourism industry, and some surreptitiously stocked by private interlopers. Largemouths themselves were originally found only from southeastern Canada down through the Great Lakes to Mexico and Florida, and no farther north on the eastern seaboard than Maryland. Nevertheless, the Florida-strain bass is not nearly as cold-resistant as northern largemouths and their genes circulating in a northern population are a potential source of massive winterkills.

For reliable big bass fishing, Florida's Lake Okeechobee, the nation's fourth largest natural lake, would be the destination of choice. Three convergent data lead to this conclusion. The gentleman who set the Lake Okeechobee record of 17 pounds, 3 ounces, in 1971, lost another bass he reported as "much larger." Secondly, Roland Martin has chosen to live on the shores of Okeechobee. He is the most successful competitive bass fisherman in North America, with a casting arm as relentless as a metronome and a faultless knowledge of the quarry. He thinks Okeechobee is the best lake in the nation for limiting out with large bass, and the most reliable winter largemouth fishery in the United States (for weeks on end, during some winters, bass fishing in the United States is largely futile except from Lake Okeechobee south). And thirdly, a scan of largemouth bass record fish, state by state, shows a suspiciously large number taken during the months of December through March. Fishing a black jig-and-porkrind eel in the deepest holes to be found in Lake Okeechobee, on the sort of day when the orange grove ranchers have all their smudge pots burning, might produce something really gross.

If you would like to catch both more and larger bass without mounting an expedition to the far southern corners of the United States, then go angling in the nearest bass lake after dark during deep summer. This simply devastating strategy can be effective during both the dark and full of the moon. The proper technique for fishing bass on a summer night is from a boat because most snakes are nocturnal. A calm lake is desirable, which means staying off the big impoundments, because you want to surface fish and that practice is ineffective in a chop. For once the method of choice should not be fly-fishing, but plug casting with a reel that will not tangle or backlash, which means you may select from spinning, spin-casting or magnetically braked bait-casting reels.

Using such equipment, I have over the years fished, with popping plugs and wobbling-gurgling baits, such as the famous Arbogast Jitterbug, only to have more experienced friends outfish me two to one, or worse. Their lure is a floating, cigar-shaped plug with a little propeller at each end. Smithwick's Devil's Horse is a classic brand made in Shreveport and sold throughout the South. They produce a whirring noise as you reel them steadily in. Do not try to be artful with twitches and pauses. Position the slowly moving boat a long cast from shore, cast the plug gently on the bankside water, then establish an unvarying track of sound across the surface. Give the bass a target to pursue. Try to fish where there is a plenitude of animal noises. Water too acidic or oxygen-deficient for frogs and insects is also inferior for bass. Talk becomes hushed at night because water carries sound so remarkably. After a time all you will hear are the little propellers, the frogs and crickets, and the irregularly recurrent *chugs* of taking bass.

Bait casting for largemouth has been an American tradition since early in the nineteenth century when a group of watchmakers in Kentucky began manufacturing the first bait-casting reels. In 1810, George Snyder reportedly made the original multiplying reel (geared down so the spool rotated many times for each turn of the handle). The best known builders of these turning-spool reels with jeweled bearings were Jonathon Meek and Benjamin Milam. The reels cost a fabulous $50.00 in those days, and were only affordable to the Gentry. Collectors now pay thousands for specimens in mint condition. Many were crafted of brass and nickel, silver, an alloy of nickel, and copper. Circa 1840 Meek made a solid silver reel for D. Vertner of Lexington, Kentucky.

These were called bait-casting reels because they cast bait, not lures. Minnows and frogs were popular for largemouth bass, but hellgrammites and juvenile crayfish were cherished when available. Bait fish necessitates soft-tipped rods so as not to catapult the bait across the river and into the trees. Our great-grandfathers used supple, 10-foot, two-handed rods until James Heddon whittled his first plug at Dowagiac Creek in Michigan, initiating a craze for casting artificial lures that continues undiminished today.

Largemouth bass are most often found in very close proximity to weed and wood, and few of us have either the deadeye accuracy or steely nerves to fish ultralight lures on wispy lines in aquatic jungles. But with 30-pound-test you can slap down a half ounce plug on top of a lily pad, shred the pad and continue your retrieve. If some *elodea* gets in your way, uproot it.

Excerpted from
McCLANE'S GAME FISH
OF NORTH AMERICA

"AIRBOURNE—LARGEMOUTH BASS"–MARK SUSINNO

"THE POOL BY THE FALLS"–ADRIANO MANOCCHIA

"And in the end, it is this kind of focus—the undiluted attention of the fisherman

on foot—that provides the most exciting bass fishing of all. The sensation of

meeting the fish on its own terms, and at close quarters, is unmatched."

BASS

& BASSIN'

George Kramer
1990

THERE ARE A FEW THINGS you can't enjoy in every state in the Union but, outside of Alaska, bass fishing isn't one of them. That availability, no doubt, may be the biggest reason that freshwater bass has become the most popular game fish in America. From coast to coast, in rivers, bayous, pits, and ponds, the bass is king and its followers are many.

The bass is also a fish with tradition. It was on this continent that some early British visitors to the Florida shore got a fishing lesson in the land of the Seminoles. Largemouth bass originally reigned in the more sluggish river systems of the East and Southeast, while their smallmouthed cousins dominated the cooler, though just as expansive, regions from the Great Lakes to what is now Tennessee. Some of the *Micropterus* genus have established their own niches in narrow ranges, whereas other species, like the Alabama spotted bass, have found new homes from Georgia to California. Black bass have endured generations of fish and fishermen, dams and pollution, transplantings and heavy harvests, bringing their own brand of selective pugnacity into the lives of hopeful fishermen.

Throughout their long residency in North America, fishermen have made ample and unusual attempts at catching bass, even though they may not always have known what they had. For instance, the term *green trout*, a misnomer for the largemouth, originated in 1773 and persisted well into the 1950s. But history, even fishing history, must have some parameters. Sportswriters often refer to the "modern era" when speaking about records and performances, and students of bass fishing might do the same.

Certainly, the 1920s might be one place to hasten in the new era—a time when baitcasting reels were commonplace and wood was the primary material in lure manufacture. Who can deny the flavorful story of Heddon Zara Spook? Produced in Michigan and first introduced in 1922, the cigar-shaped topwater bait was originally devised in Florida, where local fishermen compared its tail-walking motion to Pensacola's "girls on Zaragossa Street." Over time, the name was shortened to Zara and spook was added by the manufacturer to describe the skeleton-like rib pattern painted on the lure's sides.

Another more curious bass bait was developed during the same era. In Wisconsin in 1920 Alan P. Jones, founder of the Uncle Josh Bait Company, carved an imitation frog from a chunk of pork back fat because there was a shortage of the real thing that summer. The bait worked so well that Jones used his meat-processing company to supply the needed pig parts; he began selling the baits commercially in 1922. Having withstood the competition introduced by plastics, these pork-rind baits still catch bass as they did on Wisconsin's Jordan Lake so many years ago.

Other items have also had an impact on bass fishing. Since the introduction of the plastic worm, most notably by Nick Creme of Creme Lures, following World War II, there have been untold bass taken on these bogus crawlers, grubs, and eels. The very first ones were straight nightcrawler casts in nightcrawler colors, but since then salted, scented, and chemo-accented curl tails, ribs, pockets, and membranes have been added in limitless colors.

The arrival of graphite rods during the mid-1970s caused repercussions in bass fishing. On the one hand, no rods had ever been as light or as sensitive, and yet, many retailers were heard to mutter, "Who's going to buy a fifty-dollar fishing rod? Who's going to buy half a dozen?" Of course, the answer was not everyone. But hundreds of thousands of fishermen do. In the last 20 years, not only has there been a demand for better tackle, but also better and faster boats, stronger and thinner fishing line, and more sensitive and functional sonar. And the quest goes on.

While the chase is as intense as ever, there has been a change of heart regarding the bass. Although still revered, the bass is no longer quite the same object of machismo, where a stringer of fish was a statement of virility. The bass tournament still crowns a winner, record fish are still recorded, and the weekender lands all that he can. But often as not, the fish are offered a reprieve to battle again. We honor them.

Due to transplanting, the largemouth bass is found in every state in the continental United States, but it grows larger in a temperate environment. The "northern strain," *Micropterus salmoides salmoides*, grows to some 26 inches in length and about 15 pounds at maximum size, however, it probably averages less than 2 pounds nationwide. The Florida strain, *M. salmoides floridanus*, however, like the world record of 22 pounds 4 ounces, grows as large as 30 inches and would likely attain a weight of 24 pounds or more, given the opportunity. It eats virtually anything live that it can catch—

fish, amphibians, reptiles, rodents, or birds—in its attempt to reach that size.

The smallmouth bass, M. *dolomieui*, is found in every state except Florida and Alaska, but it is well established from the Great Lakes to the Saint Lawrence River and through the upper Mississippi, Ohio, and Tennessee river systems and in many deep, clear lakes and reservoirs from New Hampshire to California. The world record of 11 pounds 15 ounces came from Dale Hollow Reservoir in Tennessee, but in most parts of the country,

"SMALLMOUTH BASS"
—ALAN JAMES ROBINSON

a 5-pounder would be a trophy. Its smaller maw (mouth closed, its jaw does not extend past the eye) gives the fish its name. Without a distinct black lateral line down the side, the smallmouth's bronze or copper coloring has led to the nickname "brownie" or "brown fish." The smallmouth also has a broad diet, but crayfish may top the bill, followed by leeches, minnows,

and aquatic insects, depending on the locale.

The spotted bass, M. *punctulatus*, is most common in the waters of Kentucky, northern Alabama, Georgia, and Missouri, however, the world record of 9 pounds 4 ounces was established in California's Lake Perris. Sometimes referred to as a "Kentucky," the spotted bass is often found in rocky or cliff-bound areas. It is fond of crawfish and will also take all manner of minnows, shad, and fry. Although the average spot is usually under 2 pounds, it may be the most dogged of the black bass when hooked. Broken splotches of blue green above and below the lateral line give the fish its name, but its most identifiable characteristic is a patch of bristly teeth on its "tongue."

The shoal bass, M.—, is a genus without a species due to taxonomic questions over its similarity to the redeye bass. Fish identified as shoal bass have been recorded up to 8 pounds 3 ounces in Georgia, while the Alabama and Florida records are almost as large. The fish favors a fast-moving current and is found only in the limited range of three river systems—the Apalachicola in Florida, the Chattahoochee in Alabama, and the Flint in Georgia. The fish eats mostly crayfish. A colorful fish, the shoal bass sports a bronze-tinted back with greenish bands down the sides; its fins are usually a brownish red. Unlike the redeye, however, this larger fish features a prominent spot before its caudal or tail fin and another on the edge of its gill plate.

The redeye, M. *coosae*, is another fastwater black bass that prefers cool waters. It is much smaller than the shoal bass, rarely exceeding 1 pound. Its range is also limited to parts of Georgia and Tennessee. Bronze-backed with reddish fins, the redeye has distinct opaque white-and-bronze markings on the causal fin. This tiny bass graduates to a crayfish diet after growing up on terrestrial and aquatic insects.

The Suwannee bass, M. *notius*, is another of the little bass with a limited range. Favoring shoal areas in the current, it exists in the drainage of the Suwannee and Ochlockonee rivers in northern Florida and, to a small degree, in southern Georgia. The world record, taken in Florida, is 3 pounds 14 ounces, measuring under 17 inches. The thick-bodied Suwannee almost appears to be a cross between a smallmouth and a spot. It favors crayfish over any other foodstuff.

The Guadalupe bass, M. *treculi*, is a Texas native found in the headwaters of the San Antonio River, the Guadalupe River, and parts of the Brazos and upper Colorado rivers. No larger than 4 pounds and looking much like a spotted bass, this small fish is at home in shallow running waters below riffles, although it has been successful in a few reservoirs where it had existed before impounding. In rivers, the Guadalupe feeds primarily on aquatic insects, however, it will adapt to other forage when living in reservoirs such as Lake Buchanan or Lake Travis.

✦ Stream & Shore

If levels of enjoyment and dedication do not differentiate bass fishermen, then the relative pace of this fishing may. Shore fishermen, both waders and bank walkers, using all manner of tackle from artful fly rods to functional spincasters, must take the slow road to catching bass. But what a perspective this deliberate approach can provide. While the boat-riding contingent may anticipate yet another spot "down the lake," the wader, or shoreliner, is not burdened with such luxuries. His particular opportunities for success are right in front of him or at least within a few hundred feet in either direction. His measure of satisfaction, then, is just how well he can entice the bass from a relatively limited area.

Among the many methods available, the flyrodder sometimes has a marked advantage over those using "conventional" bass tackle. This is particularly true when using popping bugs or other topwaters for largemouths. In

wading a grassy flat during the spring, for instance, the flyrodder is able to make numerous presentations of his bait without ever having to retrieve the line. A spin-fisherman, by comparison, may have an effective lure in a balsa wood minnow, but he must reel it in following every cast before he can toss it again. The flyrodder merely picks up the line from the water and redirects the bug.

Of course, the real artists are those flyrodders who stalk smallmouth bass from a river or stream. Not only do they face the challenge of fooling the most wily of the black bass, they must do so in a finicky current, while mending casts and working assorted streamers, bugs, and nymphs. Unlike the static waters of the reservoir or pond, the moving water limits the fisherman's mobility in the pool or run and mutes his sensitivity to strikes. Wading takes special skills and a thoughtful plan of attack. In many ways, these smallmouth chasers are akin to the tournament pros with their selectivity in tackle and attention to detail. Self-contained, flyrodders pack everything that they might use in their vests, but even though they're all dressed up, they really have nowhere to go.

Bank walkers, unlike the tournament crowd, are not subject to any arbitrary rules about techniques or baits. There are seasoned veterans tossing spinnerbaits confidently as they circle a Texas tank. There are adventuresome youths slipping down the face of a steep Kansas pit mine, anxious to toss a live frog into the clear water. And there are those patient Californians, hunched over a brushy bank, fingering the line as they slowly inch their plastic worms along the bottom. Yet they all share a certain commonality, a certain collective focus.

If nothing else, shoreline fishing, in its many varieties, puts a premium on the entire experience not just on the predictable cast or obligatory retrieve. Every step to the fishing spot—across a marsh, under barbed wire, along rocky inclines, or over washboard roads—has much to do with making a memorable fishing trip. Who could recall the difference between one windy boat ride and another? But the shore fisherman can vividly describe snagging a crankbait in the underbrush or nearly losing a boot in the bog. And who could forget the lure hung hopelessly on an underwater snag or the sickening feeling of leaving the last pack of hooks in the trunk of the car?

And what about the elements? While not exactly fair-weather fishermen, most shoreliners are prone to angling during the milder parts of the year. But during the spring, a time when bass have moved toward the shallows (and the shoreliners), the weather forecaster offers no guarantees. High clouds may rapidly give way to thunderheads, and wet and windy times prevail. The boater may quickly escape to the boathouse or duck beneath a bridge. But the bass-fishing shoreliner must make a decision: march back through the wetlands, or hunker down and wait out the storm. More often than not, he stays put and "one more cast" leads to *one more* cast.

And in the end, it is this kind of focus— the undiluted attention of the fisherman on foot—that provides the most exciting bass fishing of all. The sensation of meeting the fish on its own terms, and at close quarters, is unmatched. Bass fishing is not long-distance surf casting, it is far more personal. In fact, it's much more like hunting quail or other upland game birds. Hiding in the brush or weed beds or beneath a pocket of lily pads, the bass is not likely to flush, rather it clings to its hideout. Understanding this trait, 'walkers and waders may move within a few feet of their quarry, able to dangle a plastic worm or a piece of pork rind or even a large nightcrawler, and have the bass strike with abandon.

Surely that is ample reward for the bass-fishing infantry.

Excerpted from
BASS FISHING—AN AMERICAN TRADITION

Adriano Manocchia ©

"ALONG THE BANK"–ADRIANO MANOCCHIA

"STRETCH OF HEAVEN"–ADRIANO MANOCCHIA

". . . a place where barefoot boys wade and fish for chubs . . .

so shallow, so open to the sky, few fishermen ever learned that in its secret stony

caverns hid a great golden-bronze treasure of a bass."

THE LORD *of*

LACKAWAXEN CREEK

Zane Grey
1908

WINDING AMONG the Blue Hills of Pennsylvania there is a swift amber stream that the Indians named Lack-a-wax-en. The literal translation no one seems to know, but it must mean, in mystical and imaginative Delaware, "the brown water that turns and whispers and tumbles." It is a little river hidden away under gray cliffs and hills black with ragged pines. It is full of mossy stones and rapid ripples.

All its tributaries, dashing white-sheeted over ferny cliffs, wine-brown where the whirling pools suck the stain from the hemlock roots, harbor the speckled trout. Wise in their generation, the black and red-spotted little beauties keep to their brooks; for, farther down, below the rush and fall, a newcomer is lord of the stream. He is an archenemy, a scorner of beauty and blood, the wolf-jawed, red-eyed, bronze-backed black bass.

A mile or so more from its mouth the Lackawaxen leaves the shelter of the hills and seeks the open sunlight and slows down to widen into long lanes that glide reluctantly over the few last restraining barriers to the Delaware. In a curve between two of these level lanes there is a place where barefoot boys wade and fish for chubs and bask on the big boulders like turtles. It is a famous hole for chubs and bright-sided shiners and sunfish. And, perhaps because it is so known, and so shallow, so open to the sky, few fishermen ever learned that in its secret stony caverns hid a great golden-bronze treasure of a bass.

In vain had many a flimsy feathered hook been flung over his lair by fly-casters and whisked gracefully across the gliding surface of his pool. In vain had many a shiny spoon and pearly minnow reflected sun glints through the watery windows of his home. In vain had many a hellgramite and frog and grasshopper been dropped in front of his broad nose.

Chance plays the star part in a fisherman's luck. One still, cloudy day, when the pool glanced dark under a leaden sky, I saw a wave that reminded me of the wake of a rolling tarpon; then followed an angry swirl, the skitter of a frantically leaping chub, and a splash that ended with a sound like the deep chung of water sharply turned by an oar.

Big bass choose strange hiding-places. They should be looked for in just such holes and rifts and shallows as will cover their backs. But to corral a six-pounder in the boy's swimming-hole was a circumstance to temper a fisherman's vanity with experience.

Thrillingly conscious of the possibilities of this pool, I studied it thoughtfully. It was a wide, shallow bend in the stream, with dark channels between submerged rocks, suggestive of underlying shelves. It had a current, too, not noticeable at first glance. And this pool looked at long and carefully, colored by the certainty of its guardian, took on an aspect most alluring to an angler's spirit. It had changed from a pond girt by stony banks, to a foam-flecked running stream, clear, yet hiding its secrets, shallow, yet full of labyrinthine watercourses. It presented problems which, difficult as they were, faded in a breath before a fisherman's optimism.

I tested my leader, changed the small hook for a large one, and selecting a white shiner fully six inches long, I lightly hooked it through the side of the upper lip. A sensation never outgrown since boyhood, a familiar mingling of strange fear and joyous anticipation, made me stoop low and tread the slippery stones as if I were stalking an Indian. I knew that a glimpse of me, or a faint jar vibrating under the water, or an unnatural ripple on its surface, would be fatal to my enterprise.

I swung the lively minnow and instinctively dropped it with a splash over a dark space between two yellow sunken stones. Out of the amber depths started a broad bar of bronze, rose and flashed into gold. A little dimpling eddying circle, most fascinating of all watery forms, appeared round where the minnow had sunk. The golden moving flash went down and vanished in the greenish gloom like a tiger stealing into a jungle. The line trembled, slowly swept out and straightened. How fraught that instant with a wild yet waiting suspense, with a thrill potent and blissful!

Did the fisherman ever live who could wait in such a moment? My arms twitched involuntarily. The bass leaped out of a flying splash, shook himself in a tussle plainly audible, and slung the hook back at me like a bullet.

In such moments one never sees the fish distinctly; excitement deranges the vision, and the picture, though impressive, is dim and dream-like. But a blind man would have known this bass to be enormous, for when he fell he cut the water as a heavy stone.

The best of fishing is that a mild philosophy attends even the greatest misfortunes. To be sure this philosophy is a delusion peculiar to fishermen. It is something that goes with the game and makes a fellow fancy he is a stoic, invulnerable to the slings and arrows of outrageous fortune.

So I went on my way upstream, cheerfully, as one who minded not at all an incident of angling practice; spiritedly as one who had seen many a big bass go by the board. The wind blew softly in my face; the purple clouds, marshaled aloft in fleets, sailed away into the gray distance; the stream murmured musically; a kingfisher poised marvelously over a pool, shot downward like a streak, to rise with his quivering prey; birds sang in the willows and daisies nodded in the fields; misty veils hung low in the hollows; all those attributes of nature, poetically ascribed by anglers to be the objects of their full content, were about me.

"TAIL WALKING—SMALLMOUTH BASS"–MARK SUSINNO

I found myself thinking about my two brothers, Cedar and Reddy for short, both anglers of long standing and some reputation. It was a sore point with me and a stock subject for endless disputes that they just never could appreciate my superiority as a fisherman. Brothers are singularly prone to such points of view. So when I thought of them I felt the incipient stirring of a mighty plot. It occurred to me that the iron-mouthed old bass, impregnable of jaw as well as of stronghold, might be made to serve a turn. And all the afternoon the thing grew and grew in my mind.

Luck favoring me, I took home a fair string of fish, and remarked to my brothers that the conditions for fishing the stream were favorable. Thereafter morning on morning my eyes sought the heavens, appealing for a cloudy day. At last one came, and I invited Reddy to go with me. With childish pleasure, that would have caused weakness in any but an unscrupulous villain, he eagerly accepted. He looked over a great assortment of tackle, and finally selected a five-ounce Leonard bait-rod carrying a light reel and fine line. When I thought of what would happen if Reddy hooked that powerful bass an unholy glee fastened upon my soul.

We never started out that way together, swinging rods and pails, but old associations were awakened. We called up the time when we had left the imprints of bare feet on the country roads; we lived over many a boyhood adventure by a running stream. And at last we wound up on the never threadbare question as to the merit and use of tackle.

"I always claimed," said Reddy, "that a fisherman should choose tackle for a day's work after the fashion of a hunter in choosing his gun. A hunter knows what kind of game he's after, and takes a small or large caliber accordingly. Of course a fisherman has more rods than there are calibers of guns, but the rule holds. Now today I have brought this light rod and thin line because I don't need weight. I don't see why you've brought that heavy rod. Even a two-pound bass would be a great surprise up this stream."

"You're right," I replied, "but I sort of lean to possibilities. Besides, I'm fond of this rod. You know I've caught a half-dozen bass of from five to six pounds with it. I wonder what you would do if you hooked a big one on the delicate thing."

"Do?" ejaculated my brother. "I'd have a fit! I might handle a big bass in deep water with this outfit, but here in this shallow stream with its rocks and holes I couldn't. And that is the reason so few big bass are taken from the Delaware. We know they are there, great lusty fellows! Every day in season we hear some tale of woe from some fisherman. 'Hooked a big one—broke this—broke that—got under a stone.' That's why no five- or six-pound bass are taken from shallow, swift, rock-bedded streams on light tackle."

When we reached the pool I sat down and began to fumble with my leader. How generously I let Reddy have the first cast! My iniquity carried me to the extreme of bidding him steal softly and stoop low. I saw a fat chub swinging in the air; I saw it alight to disappear in a churning commotion of the water, and I heard Reddy's startled, "Gee!"

Hard upon his exclamation followed action of striking swiftness. A shrieking reel, willow wand of a rod wavering like a buggy-whip in the wind, curving splashes round a foam-lashed swell, a crack of dry wood, a sound as of a banjo string snapping, a sharp splash, then a heavy sullen souse; these, with Reddy standing voiceless, eyes glaring on a broken rod and limp trailing line, were the essentials of the tragedy.

Somehow the joke did not ring true when Reddy waded ashore calm and self-contained, with only his burning eyes to show how deeply he felt. What he said to me in a quiet voice must not, owing to family pride, go on record. It most assuredly would not be an addition to the fish literature of the day.

But he never mentioned the incident to Cedar, which omission laid the way open for my further machinations. I realized that I should have tried Cedar first. He was one of those white-duck-pants-on-a-dry-rock sort of a fisherman, anyway. And in due time I had him wading out toward the center of that pool.

I always experienced a painful sensation while watching Cedar cast. He must have gotten his style from a Delsartian school. One moment he resembled Ajax defying the lightning and the next he looked like the fellow who stood on a monument, smiling at grief. And not to mention pose, Cedar's execution was wonderful. I have seen him cast a frog a mile—but the frog had left the hook. It was remarkable to see him catch his hat, and terrifying to hear the language he used at such an ordinary angling event. It was not safe to be in his vicinity, but if you turned your back an instant, his flying hook would have a fiendish affinity for your trousers, and it was not beyond his powers to swing you kicking out over the stream. All of which, considering the frailties of human nature and of fishermen, could be forgiven; he had, however, one great fault impossi-

ble to overlook, and it was that he made more noise than a playful hippopotamus.

I hoped, despite all these things, that the big bass would rise to the occasion. He did rise. He must have recognized the situation of his life. He spread the waters of his shallow pool and accommodatingly hooked himself.

Cedar's next graceful move was to fall off the slippery stone on which he had been standing and to go out of sight. His hat floated downstream; the arched tip of his rod came up, then his arm, and his dripping shoulders and body. He yelled like a savage and pulled on the fish hard enough to turn a tuna in the air. The big bass leaped three times, made a long shoot with his black dorsal fin showing, and then, with a lunge, headed for some place remote from there. Cedar ploughed after him, sending water in sheets, and then he slipped, wildly swung his arms, and fell again.

I was sinking to the ground, owing to unutterable and overpowering sensations of joy, when a yell and a commotion in the bushes heralded the appearance of Reddy.

"Hang on, Cedar! Hang on!" he cried, and began an Indian war-dance.

The few succeeding moments were somewhat blurred because of my excess of emotion. When I returned to consciousness Cedar was wading out with a hookless leader, a bloody shin, and a disposition utterly and irretrievably ruined.

"Put up a job on me!" he roared.

Thereafter during the summer each of us made solitary and sneaking expeditions, bent on the capture of the lord of the Lackawaxen. And somehow each would return to find the other two derisively speculative as to what caused his clouded brow. Leader on leader went to grace the rocks of the old bronze

warrior's home. At length Cedar and Reddy gave up, leaving the pool to me. I fed more than one choice shiner to the bass and more than once he sprang into the air to return my hook.

Summer and autumn passed; winter came to lock the Lackawaxen in icy fetters; I fished under Southern skies where lagoons and moss-shaded waters teemed with great and gamy fish, but I never forgot him. I knew that when the season rolled around, when a June sun warmed the cold spring-fed Lackawaxen, he would be waiting for me.

Who was it spoke of the fleeting of time? Obviously he had never waited for the opening of the fishing season. But at last the tedious time was like the water that has passed. And then I found I had another long wait. Brilliant June days without a cloud were a joy to live, but worthless for fishing. Through all that beautiful month I plodded up to the pool, only to be unrewarded. Doubt began to assail me. Might not the ice, during the spring break-up, have scared him from the shallow hole? No. I felt that not even a rolling glacier could have moved him from his subterranean home.

Often as I reached the pool I saw fishermen wading down the stream, and on these occasions I sat on the bank and lazily waited for the intruding disturbers of my peace to pass on. Once, the first time I saw them, I had an agonizing fear that one of the yellow-helmeted, khaki-coated anglers would hook my bass. The fear, of course, was groundless, but I could not help human feelings. The idea of that grand fish rising to a feathery imitation of a bug or a lank dead bait had nothing in my experience to warrant its consideration. Small, lively bass, full of play, fond of chasing their golden shadows, and belligerent and hungry, were ready to fight and eat whatever swam into their ken. But a six-pound bass, slow to reach such weight in swift-running water, was old and wise and full of years. He did not feed often, and when he did he wanted a live fish big enough for a good mouthful. So, with these facts to soothe me I rested my fears, and got to look humorously at the invasions of the summer-hotel fishers.

They came wading, slipping, splashing downstream, blowing like porpoises, slapping at the water with all kinds of artificial and dead bait. And they called to me in a humor actuated by my fishing garb and the rustic environment:

"Hey, Rube! Ketchin' any?"

I said the suckers were bitin' right pert.

"What d'you call this stream?"

I replied, giving the Indian name.

"Lack-a-what? Can't you whistle it? Lack-awhacken? You mean Lack-afishing."

"Lack-arotten," joined in another.

"Do you live here?" questioned a third.

I modestly said yes.

"Why don't you move?" Whereupon they all laughed and pursued the noisy tenor of their way downstream, pitching their baits around.

"Say, fellows," I shouted after them, "are you training for the casting tournament in Madison Square Garden or do you think you're playing lacrosse?"

The laugh that came back proved the joke on them, and that it would be remembered as part of the glorious time they were having.

July brought the misty, dark, lowering days. Not only did I find the old king at home on these days, but just as contemptuous of hooks and leaders as he had been the summer before. About the middle of the month he stopped giving me paralysis of the heart; that is to say, he quit rising to my tempting chubs and shiners. So I left him alone to rest, to rust out hooks and grow less suspicious.

By the time August came, the desire to call on him again was well-nigh irresistible. But I waited, and fished the Delaware, and still waited. I would get him when the harvest moon was full. Like all the old moss-backed denizens of the shady holes, he would come out for a last range over the feeding shoals. At length a morning broke humid and warm, almost dark as twilight, with little gusts of fine rain. Of all days this was the day! I chose a stiff rod, a heavy silk line, a stout brown leader, and a large hook. From my bait box I took two five-inch red catfish, the little "stone-rollers" of the Delaware, and several long shiners. Thus equipped I sallied forth.

The walk up the towpath, along the canal with its rushes and sedges, across the meadows white with late-blooming daisies, lost nothing because of its familiarity. When I reached the pool I saw in the low water near shore several small bass scouting among the schools of min- nows. I did not want these pugnacious fellows to kill my bait, so, procuring a hellgramite from under a stone, I put it on my hook and promptly caught two of them, and gave the other a scare he would not soon forget.

I decided to try the bass with one of his favorite shiners. With this trailing in the water I silently waded out, making not so much as a ripple. The old familiar oppression weighed on my breast; the old throbbing boyish excitement tingled through my blood. I made a long cast and dropped the shiner lightly. He went under and then came up to swim about on the sur- face. This was a sign that made my heart leap. Then the water bulged, and a black bar shot across the middle of the long shiner. He went down out of sight, the last gleams of his divided brightness fading slowly. I did not need to see the little shower of silver scales floating up to know that the black bar had

been the rounded nose of the old bass and that he had taken the shiner across the middle. I struck hard, and my hook came whistling at me. I had scored a clean miss.

I waded ashore very carefully, sat down on a stone by my bait pail, and meditated. Would he rise again? I had never know him to do so twice in one day. But then there had never been occasion. I bethought me of the "stone-rollers" and thrilled with certainty. Whatever he might resist, he could not resist one of those little red catfish. Long ago, when he was only a three- or four-pounder, roaming the deep eddies and swift rapids of the Delaware, before he had isolated himself to a peaceful old age in this quiet pool, he must have poked his nose under many a stone, with red eyes keen for one of those dainty morsels.

My excitation thrilled itself out to the calm assurance of the experienced fisherman. I firmly fastened on one of the catfish and stole out into the pool. I waded farther than ever before; I was careful but confident. Then I saw the two flat rocks dimly shining. The water was dark as it rippled by, gurgling softly; it gleamed with lengthening shadows and glints of amber.

I swung the catfish. A dull flash of sunshine seemed to come up to meet him. The water swirled and broke with a splash. The broad black head of the bass just skimmed the surface; his jaws opened wide to take in the bait; he turned and flapped a huge spread tail on the water.

Then I struck with all the power the tackle would stand. I felt the hook catch solidly as if in a sunken log. Swift as flashing light the bass leaped. The drops of water hissed and the leader whizzed. But the hook held. I let out one exultant yell. He did not leap again. He dashed to the right, then the left, in bursts of surprising speed. I had hardly warmed to the work when he settled down and made for the dark channel between the yellow rocks. My triumph was to be short-lived. Where was the beautiful spectacular surface fight I expected of him? Cunning old monarch! He laid his great weight dead on the line and lunged for his sunken throne. I held him with a grim surety of the impossibility of stopping him. How I longed for

"LARGEMOUTH WITH LILY PADS"–ALAN JAMES ROBINSON

deep, open water! The rod bent, the line strained and stretched. I removed my thumb and the reel sang one short shrill song. Then the bass was as still as the rock under which he had gone.

I had never dislodged a big bass from under a stone, and I saw herein further defeat; but I persevered, waded to different angles, and working all the tricks of the trade. I could not drag the fish out, nor pull the hook loose. I sat down on a stone and patiently waited for a long time, hoping he would come out of his own accord.

As a final resort, precedent to utter failure, I waded out. The water rose to my waist, then to my shoulders, my chin, and all but covered my raised face. When I reached the stone under which he had planted himself I stood in water about four feet deep. I saw my leader, and tugged upon it, and kicked under the stone, all to no good.

Then I calculated I had a chance to dislodge him if I could get my arm under the shelf. So down I went, hat, rod, and all. The current was just swift enough to lift my feet, making my task more difficult. At the third trial I got my hand on a sharp corner of stone and held fast. I ran my right hand along the leader, under the projecting slab of rock, till I touched the bass. I tried to get hold of him, but had to rise for air.

I dove again. The space was narrow, so narrow that I wondered how so large a fish could have gotten there. He had gone under sidewise, turned, and wedged his dorsal fin, fixing himself as solidly as the rock itself. I pulled frantically till I feared I would break the leader.

When I floundered up to breathe again the thought occurred to me that I could rip him with my knife and, by taking the life out of him, loosen the powerful fin so he could be dragged out. Still, much as I wanted him I could not do that. I resolved to make one more fair attempt. In a quick determined plunge I secured a more favorable hold for my left hand and reached under with my right. I felt his whole long length and I could not force a finger behind him anywhere. The gill toward me was shut tight like a trap door. But I got a thumb and forefinger fastened to his lip. I tugged till a severe cramp numbed my hand; I saw red and my head whirled; a noise roared in my ears. I stayed until one more second would have made me a drowning man, then rose gasping and choking.

I broke off the leader close to the stone and waded ashore. I looked back at the pool, faintly circled by widening ripples. What a great hole and what a grand fish! I was glad I did not get him and knew I would never again disturb his peace.

So I took my rod and pail and the two little bass, and brushed the meadow daisies, and threaded the familiar green-lined towpath toward home.

Excerpted from
TALES OF FRESH-WATER FISHING

"LUNCH—LARGEMOUTH BASS"–MARK SUSINNO

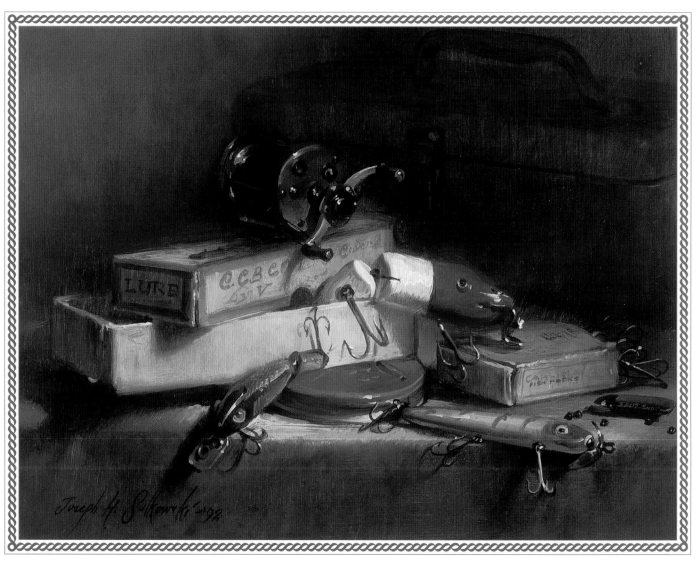

"DAD'S TACKLE BOX"–JOSEPH SULKOWSKI

"Then, in 1958, he and his wife, Ann, bought five dollars' worth of lead and some

polar-bear hair and began to make lures on the kitchen table. Tom carved and

molded the jig bodies, Ann painted them, and then he tied the white tails."

CATCHING BASS

ON TELEVISION

Jimmy Carter
1988

"WHEN I WAS GOVERNOR of Georgia, I fished a few times in the Walter F. George Reservoir—or Lake Eufaula, as it is known by all Alabamians and most Georgians from the western part of the state. After one of these trips, some of the news stories reported—accurately—that my catch had been very small.

Within a few days I received in the mail a small box of lures and a book entitled *Tom Mann's Methods for Catching Bass*. The gift was from the book's author and recent winner of the national B.A.S.S. tournament at Lake Kissimmee, Florida. At that time, in 1972, the Bass Anglers Sportsman Society was a well-established and widely known organization among all warm-water fishermen. A few years later, I was to welcome Tom Mann to the Oval Office to receive a presidential award as the outstanding small businessman of the nation.

Tom had grown up as a farm boy with a life very similar to mine. He'd plowed a mule, fished for "horney heads" and small bream in the tiny branches, for catfish and eels in muddy and rising creeks when it was too wet to work in the fields, gigged suckers during

their spawning runs, and then graduated to plug fishing for bass in nearby ponds.

Fishing became his greatest passion. As a schoolboy his goal was to be a conservation officer, a professional guide, or to get a job with a fishing lure manufacturer. After high school he worked for a time in a cotton mill, deliberately choosing the night and early-morning shifts so that he would have plenty of time to fish in the afternoons. After serving in the Korean War, he came home to a job as an Alabama game and fish biologist. Then, in 1958, he and his wife, Ann, bought five dollars' worth of lead and some polar-bear hair and began to make lures on the kitchen table. Tom carved and molded the jig bodies, Ann painted them, and then he tied the white tails.

Tom caught so many fish on his innovative designs that he began to sell them to some of the neighbors. The business grew, and soon the Manns were making more income from the lures than from his state job. They bought an entire polar-bear hide for $800, used it all, and shifted to other more readily available materials. Within a few years, more than a hundred employees were producing the various lures that Tom devised, and his prowess as a successful fisherman became known through competitions, from numerous articles in outdoor magazines, and an aggressive public relations campaign. Among bass fishermen, he was preeminent.

He won a number of fishing tournaments and continued to expand his various business enterprises, all centered around fishing. In 1969, using his Heathkit circuits, he began to produce a sonic depth-finder that was relatively inexpensive and able to operate in a fast-moving boat with a minimum of interference from the motor or water noises. Under the Hummingbird brand, many thousands of these devices were sold to the rapidly expanding number of fishermen who knew that the bottom configuration of lakes was a vital clue to the most likely spots for fish. Thanks to this device, they could at times actually see schools of fish on the electronic screen.

I watched Tom Mann catch fish on many television programs and tried to put his fishing techniques into practice on my own excursions in the warm waters of Georgia. By the time he came to the White House to be recognized for his success in business, I was eager to ply him with questions. However, we had no chance to talk during our busy schedules that day. Later, when my term as President was over, I was delighted to receive an invitation from him for a day's fishing.

On the day before my visit I called him just to make sure that all the arrangements were understood, ending our conversation by saying eagerly, "Okay, I'll be leaving here at six o'clock in the morning."

"DEEP COVER—LARGEMOUTH BASS"–MARK SUSINNO

There was some hesitation, and then Tom said gently, "Mr. President, you'll get here too early. It's only a fifty-mile drive, and don't forget we're an hour behind you across the river in Alabama. The older I get the more I realize that the fish will still be biting after sunup."

The next morning, an hour later than originally planned, I traveled westward from Plains through a heavy fog, crossed the Chattahoochee River, followed the signs north of Eufaula directing me to Fish World, and drove up in front of a beautiful mansion just a few yards from Tom's large freshwater aquarium. Tom and Ann welcomed me with a big breakfast of cheese grits, country ham and sausage, scrambled eggs, fresh-baked buttermilk biscuits, mayhew jelly and pear preserves, and hot coffee. When I complimented Ann on their lovely home, she said, "We were very proud when we built it, but we don't live here. A few years ago we went up the road to spend one night at the old house on our farm and never moved back. Now we just use this big house for office space and for special occasions like this."

The Manns, obviously full partners, brought me up-to-date on the latest developments in their business enterprises. They had sold both Mann Lures and the electronics company, but they and their children were still inventing new lures, manufacturing plastic worms, and publishing an outdoor magazine for children. The Manns were especially excited about expanding Fish World to include an eighteen-hole fishing course for young people which Tom was building in the lake just behind the house. Tom still entered some of the major bass tournaments just to keep his name before the public, but claimed he lacked the time and was not in good enough physical shape to be a top competitor. Nevertheless, he had just signed a contract for a new television series, for which he would begin filming twenty-six segments early in the summer.

After breakfast the fog was still too thick to move safely on the big lake, so Tom suggested that we try out some of his experimental lures on the pond across the road. "I've got a new plastic worm with a tail copied from the design of a common Indian arrowhead we find around here, and it is a lot simpler to use, has great action, and really catches fish. Because it wiggles so much, I'll probably call it the Hawaii Worm," he told me.

In the twenty-acre reservoir Tom had used his own bulldozer to scoop out deep holes, piling up the dirt to create many small islands. He suggested that I use one of my favorite lures while he tied on one of his new ones, a "walker" that he had named Hard Worm.

I fished hard with a five-inch Rapala, and he began to catch bass regularly. With a grin, he finally threw me one of his lures. My fishing improved immediately. After a half hour or so, we shifted to his new plastic worm. When pulled steadily through the water, the tail wiggled vigorously. "You don't have to know any tricks," said Tom. "Just throw it out, let it sink to the depth you want it, and crank it back in slowly."

I had as many strikes as he, but he caught two or three times as many bass. Tom held his rod almost vertical, was extremely sensitive to any nibble, and, with a quick flick of his powerful wrist and a half turn on the reel handle, could almost instantly set the hook firmly in the fish's mouth. I have noticed that most fishermen, including me, use a much slower movement of the entire arm to get as much leverage.

Some have to use so much body movement that they almost fall out of the boat when they set the hook.

Within an hour the fog lifted enough to move to Lake Eufaula. We had caught about thirty nice bass. I kept only one; after a photograph I carried it to the water's edge and released it too.

At the boat landing on the lake we talked to several fishermen, all of whom reported that the fish had just not been biting that morning or for the last few days. None of them had caught a fish. Tom was not discouraged, saying quietly, "We may be able to find a few."

As we moved away from the pier, my fishing partner commented that now, in the middle of May, most bass away from the immediate shoreline would likely be found at a depth of around ten feet, moving an average of five feet deeper each month as the water warmed up through the late spring and summer. We would first stay out in the lake and try plastic worms, tied twelve to sixteen inches below a half an ounce of lead weight, fishing the relatively shallow submerged banks around the old riverbed (the bottom of which at that time was about seventy feet deep).

A large flock of Canada geese was flying around the islands in the lake, some of the birds on the water with several goslings. "A lot of them over-winter here now," Tom said, "and one of their favorite nesting places is on the small islands in my ponds. They're protected from most of the foxes and raccoons, and the survival rate seems to be pretty high." We also watched several osprey that circled overhead, surveying the lake for fish from the tops of the dead trees. This beautiful bird, as big as some eagles with its five-foot wingspan, had almost been eradicated by the extensive use of the pesticide DDT, now banned in our country. We were delighted to see that now it was coming back. At one point, fishing near a steel tower supporting a shallow metal saucer, we saw an osprey nest with two adults perched on its edge. The game and fish rangers were trying the tower as an experimental nesting place, and it seemed to be working well.

Tom and I fished all the rest of the day except for a brief stop in a shady place for lunch. I learned a lot that I had never known before. It seemed that the key to Tom's success was an intimate knowledge of the lake bottom and an uncanny ability to read the depth-finder results. In the middle of the lake it all looked the same to me, but as he explained from his own memory, using the depth-finder on occasion to illustrate a point, each of his casts was placed to take advantage of the configuration of the bottom. We threaded our lures along old ditches, through and across standing and fallen timber, across grass flats that would be exposed if the lake level had dropped a few feet, and up and down the steep slopes of the original riverbank.

Although our rig was relatively weedless without any hook exposed, we lost a lot of plastic worms in the thick underwater brush. "This is why we sell about four million dollars' worth of these a year," Tom said. "You have to put the worms in the rough places to catch fish. They're still the cheapest and best lure to use. Eighty-five percent of the tournament bass are caught on plastic worms."

Each time we caught a fish in a new location away from the shore we threw a small marker buoy over the side, then circled it and fished the area thoroughly. Tom caught his fourth fish before I ever landed one. He was very gentle with his advice, but I watched him closely and tried to copy what he did. Since a few bass were taking shad near the surface, we tried some spinner bait and the Hard Worm, but the plastic worm on the bottom was what the fish wanted.

We also fished some in the coves. I caught a few, and again the plastic worm was the most effective lure. The only strike we had on spinner bait was from a ten-foot alligator, when Tom pulled the lure too close in front of his nose.

I asked Tom a lot of questions about the fishing tournaments. Even he was amazed at how large they had become. "I'll be fishing in a 'megabucks' tournament later this year. There will be two hundred contestants, and the entrance fee for each of us is five thousand dollars, with sixty prizes in all." When I asked him what chances he would have of at least winning his $5,000 back, he thought a while before answering: "About ninety percent."

Then he added, "Next month I'll be in the Lake Okeechobee tournament, one of my favorites because it's managed well and there are more bass per acre there than anywhere else I know. It's a lot better to compete when everyone can catch some fish.

"I remember one year we had a tournament at the West Point reservoir farther up the Chattahoochee, which is usually a fine place to fish. The temperature dropped overnight to thirty-nine degrees, and the fish just wouldn't bite. There were two hundred contestants, and only one fish was caught in three days. On the other hand, I've seen a hundred and thirty-nine pounds of bass caught by one fisherman here in Lake Eufaula. My top in a tournament is ninety-six pounds, but fishing with a friend

in 1972, we took a hundred and fifty-five pounds of bass in one day. The top seventeen averaged over seven pounds, with the biggest one a little over thirteen pounds."

"With all the tournament fishermen, it seems that the bass population would soon be depleted on the more popular reservoirs," I commented.

"We used to kill most of the fish, but now there is a two-ounce penalty if a dead one is brought in to be weighed. We're very careful to keep them alive, because a dead fish might cost you the big prize. I would estimate that ninety-five percent of the bass we catch in tournaments are released and survive. It's a big improvement, and we feel better about it."

Around sunset, clouds began rolling in from the west and we could see lightning in the distance. It was time to return to the landing—the end of a fine day with one of America's greatest fishermen.

On the way in he asked me, "Would you be willing to come back next year and join me in making one of my television programs?"

I thought about it. "I wouldn't want millions of people to see how many more bass you catch!" I concluded.

Tom was ready for me. "You bring your fly rod, I'll fish with my spinning outfit, and if there is any difference we can blame it on the tackle." I agreed to work out a mutually convenient date.

This is the kind of invitation I never forget, and so the next summer I was back with Tom Mann again. Along with my bait-casting outfit I had my #5 fly rod, a floating line, and a good selection of flies that had proven effective with bass. We first had a few words with the television crews, who would have their cameras at strategic places on the shore and in a boat that would stay as close as possible to Tom and me. He and I were outfitted with microphones on our shirt fronts and a small transmitter in our pockets so that our comments could be recorded by the technicians.

By noon the temperature was 105 degrees in the shade, and all of us were soaking with sweat. Some of the television camera batteries were damaged by the heat and there were a number of interruptions in their recording of our activities, but we didn't let let this interfere with either our conversation or our fishing. Using a small deer-hair fly on the surface, I was catching more bass than Tom with his spinning tackle, although his were somewhat bigger. In the meantime we talked about our early boyhood days, fishing tournaments, and my fly-fishing experiences in different streams around the world. For lunch we ate beenie-weenies, Vienna sausage, cheese, and crackers in the boat under the shade of a large pine tree, continuing our conversation for the benefit of the television crew.

Almost nine months later the program was telecast, and Tom sent me a videotape for my library. The size of the audience was amazing. Everywhere I went, people would let me know they had seen Tom Mann and me fishing together. And all the comments were friendly. In more ways than one this was a media experience quite different from those of my life in the political world.

Excerpted from
AN OUTDOOR JOUNAL

"My father was very sure about certain matters pertaining to the universe.

To him, all good things—trout as well as eternal salvation—come by grace

and grace comes by art and art does not come easy."

—Norman Maclean, "A River Runs Through It"

PART II
TROUT

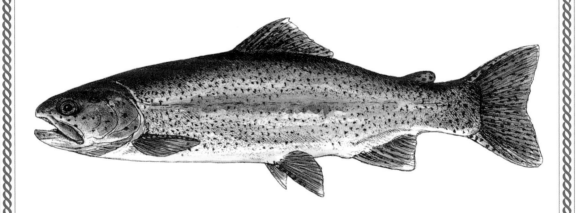

RAINBOW TROUT
Oncorhynchus mykiss

"WHERE TRANQUIL WATERS BEGIN"–ADRIANO MANOCCHIA

"The fisherman begins as a boy, young and green and eager. He is all enthusiasm

and has not had time to learn any of the bad habits that fishermen pick up easily

and discard with great pain. . . .This is the spring of a fisherman's life."

A FISHERMAN'S

SEASONS

Geoffrey Norman
1981

WHEN YOU THINK of fishing, you almost inevitably think in seasonal images. The fisherman is nearly as alert to the seasons as the poet. He thinks of spring hatches, summer doldrums, and fall runs. Every fishing story is given a seasonal background. One of the finest works in the literature of fishing is a tetralogy by Roderick Haig-Brown called, simply, *Fisherman's Spring, Fisherman's Summer, Fisherman's Fall* and *Fisherman's Winter*. To the fisherman, Haig-Brown is not so much using a literary device as thinking about his sport in the obvious way.

So it is convenient to think of the fisherman's life using seasonal metaphor. The fisherman begins as a boy, young and green and eager. He is all enthusiasm and has not had time to learn any of the bad habits that fishermen pick up easily and discard with great pain—fish hogging, for instance. And lying.

This is the spring of a fisherman's life. Perhaps the best thing about it is that there is time to fish, which does not seem like so much to a boy. A surplus resource is nothing special to its owner; probably no Arab holds oil in intrinsically high esteem. But time is precious to the adult fisherman, as the boy will soon learn. *No fisherman ever fishes as much as he wants to*—this is the first great law of fishing, and it explains a world of otherwise inexplicable behavior. . . .

But where does a boy begin? How does he get started?

Almost all fisherman start fishing as boys. Most learn from a grown man, usually their father, sometimes a relative or friend, and occasionally an older boy, a pal. Hardly anyone learns to fish absolutely alone or from a paid instructor, the way one might learn, say, to ski. Today there are several good fishing schools run by tackle manufacturers or famous fishermen. The schools are probably the answer for an adult who is just starting out; after a certain age it is more comfortable, better for the self-esteem, to keep things on a professional basis. But if you are a boy, it is better to learn from somebody older, and best of all to learn from your father. It is one thing you will be able to share across later generational conflicts. Fishing and its values are more or less constant.

Every fisherman I have spoken to on the subject says that he started fishing in his mind before he ever went out on the water. Perhaps he saw his father's tackle, stored neatly in a closet or study or workshop, and admired it the way a boy admires those material things that speak to him of manhood: razors, pipes, fine leather billfolds, expensive wristwatches. There is a message in fishing tackle. You need only to witness the passion it excites in grown men to believe that. Boys can feel the mystery, the tug, as well.

So a boy might start his life as a fisherman by putting together a tackle box. It is most likely a small metal thing, better suited to carry nails, screws, and staples and extremely vulnerable to rust. In it he stores those random pieces of equipment he has been able to accumulate. Some of it is gear that his father has discarded, and some he has bought on his own. Some merely appears along the way, which is an unexplained property of fishing tackle known to every fisherman who has ever lived.

I can still remember my own metal tackle box. It stayed in a safe corner of my closet, except when I brought it out to clean and rearrange its contents—which was almost nightly the first year I owned it. I had a handful of rubber-legged popping bugs for panfish, some leaders that I had tied up according to the formulas in a magazine article, a screwdriver, a pair of needle-nosed pliers, some Mucilin line dressing, and a homemade stringer. There was a scout knife that I had sharpened on a kitchen Carborundum, a pair of dime-store imitation aviator's glasses, a

Chap Stick, and a bottle of 6-12 insect repellent. I was ready long before my father asked me to go fishing with him. . . .

A boy whose father fished only for trout would naturally have a different box, full of old flies with flattened hackles and wets that had been cast and soaked until they were coming apart. Such a boy would spend time in the kitchen, at the stove, holding those mashed flies over the escaping steam of a hot kettle. If the damage was not too severe, that would restore the flies to a usable condition. He would probably have more odds and ends in the box than the boy whose father fished for bass or pike; the trout fisherman tends to collect miscellany. He buys gadgets to take the temperature of streams and measure the thickness of leaders and pump the stomachs of the fish he catches— and then, the next season, he gets rid of everything in his vest except for one fly box and a spool of tippet. When a trout fisherman feels the urge to simplify, something like a purge follows. So his young son inherits all sorts of specialized devices: gadgets for tying knots in the last ten minutes of twilight, and leader straighteners attached to spring-loaded spools. His tackle box may look more like something that belongs to a seamstress than to a fisherman.

But a boy's tackle box is not a real measure of anything except his desire to fish. The urge to equip is endemic in fisherman, and it reveals itself at an early age. It cannot be extinguished, only disciplined and tempered. . . .

So . . . let's say there is a young boy whose father is a fisherman and who has therefore collected a metal carpenter's box full of cast-off tackle, supplemented by a few items he has bought on his own. He is knowledgeable in an untutored fashion. He probably knows about shooting heads and double hauls before he has even caught his first bluegill on a worm. Above all, he wants to go fishing.

Why? Well, let's just say because boys will be boys and let it go at that. Whenever you poke around motive, you come to a point beyond which everything is speculative and unverifiable. Fisherman fish. They have been doing it for a long time. Not many of them turn out too badly, and with most, fishing is their worst vice.

Most fishing is done with bait. It is the best way to catch fish. It is also the best way to learn how to catch fish with artificial flies and lures. So it is good and proper that most boys, when they start fishing, use bait. One hopes and expects that they will graduate to artificials, just as they will graduate from the sports and the comics to the front page and Joseph Kraft, from R. L. Stevenson to Ernest Hemingway, from Playboy to real women. But there is no need to rush things.

There are all kinds of bait: worms, grasshoppers, crickets, hellgrammites, minnows. Every now and then you'll hear about small mice being used. Or frogs. Even birds. Anything that fish eat in nature can be used for bait, and that means almost anything. I once found a nine-inch water moccasin in the stomach of a bass.

Highbrows may sniff at bait fishing and pass it off as boring, unimaginative, and somehow not quite civilized and fitting. Too many young fisherman who come from the cities believe that the path from Orvis to the Battenkill is Euclidian, a line of no depth and no width from which one does not deviate. To such a boy, brown trout have simply been bred to take Quill Gordons. It is what they do. For him, taking fish is a sterile matter of technique, not a question of slipping unobtrusively into the great chain of life and predation and living briefly by those ancient terms. Fishing does not have to begin with a Light Cahill on the Beaverkill and end with a Jock Scott on the Restigouche. Bait is the place to start, and there is no shame in going back to it from time to time. Snobs are made, not born, and most boys are happy to fish with bait and gather their own. It is a kind of initiation. They learn about things like coffee grounds for keeping worms and a cardboard box with a forty-watt bulb for raising crickets. There is more to bait than buying it in waxed containers.

If you believe that fishing is, among many other things, an avenue to a mature appreciation of nature, you would be pressed hard to defend an opposition to bait. There is much to be learned in a lowly worm bed, not least that smell that is the first whiff most suburban boys ever get of fecund, decaying earth where the end and beginning of life are joined. Grasshoppers are more fun to gather than worms, calling for finesse and technique. If you move too slowly, you will never catch one; but if you use too much force, you will damage or kill those that you do catch. You must be quick but delicate. Catching grasshoppers can be as much fun as fishing with them. By the time a young fisherman leaves the grassy fields and heads for a stream, he almost always has more grasshoppers than he needs, and his fingers are stained with "tobacco juice."

So, with his metal box full of tackle, an old tin can full of coffee grounds and night crawlers, and a rod of some sort, our boy is ready to go fishing, if he can find someone to take him or someplace to go. Let's say he starts out by going with some other boys to a nearby lake or pond, river or creek, bay or bayou . . . .

The best fish to start with, though, is not a trout. Boys should learn about trout after they have learned about girls. Trout, and trout rivers, are sensuous and unpredictable. They frustrate more than they reward, and they have a way of making you feel inadequate. The place to start is with panfish.

For a boy, panfish are as abundant as time. They are not particular about what they eat, and they make fine eating (as the name implies) themselves. They live in all kinds of accessible water. They can survive fishing pressure and the unavoidable pollution that goes with even the best-scrubbed version of modern life. It is as difficult to conceive of panfish as a threatened species as it is to imagine the extinction of armadillos or jackrabbits. Panfish have good shape and color. They are scrappy enough to be justly labeled game fish, and they are not especially temperamental. You can use several different techniques to catch panfish: flies, spinning lures, and all sorts of bait.

Bluegills, yellow perch, crappie—these are all boys' fish. There are plenty of grown men who fish for them with something approaching lust, but they are stalemated fisherman who have never grown in the sport, meat fisherman, generally, for whom the mystery has long since died. Even in fishing you must find a way to grow.

So boys start out on panfish, using crickets or worms. The first fish is not to be believed. He

is kept alive on a stringer that is hauled out of the water for repeated study, then lowered reverently into the water again. Then raised for another look. First catch. It could not be more lovely: the faint yellow or red of the breast; the

dark ears leading off the gill plates; the puckered mouth; the sturdy compact body: the smell that is earth and water and something else, something that won't wash off easily. A fine mystery, those small fish. Just right for a boy.

It is important for a boy to be able to catch something. Boys do not see the virtues of a strictly contemplative exercise. Any number of fathers have ruined fishing for their sons by starting them on difficult bass or trout

water. The thing seems hard to begin with—all that technique and complicated jargon—and when you don't catch any fish, it becomes another tedious chore, like cutting the grass or washing the car. A boy who starts this way may get discouraged and quit for good.

But all boys can master the rudimentary techniques required for taking panfish. And since the fish are cooperative, the boy who genuinely likes fishing will soon bring home full stringers. It is a grand feeling for a boy to provide supper for his family by his wits and skill. But even that pales eventually, and the boy begins thinking about bigger fish and more exotic techniques. It is a passage of sorts, though the boy isn't likely to reflect on that very

much. But if he has decided to move up from simple bait fishing for panfish to something else—say, casting popping bugs for bass—he is acknowledging another fundamental fishing truth: *There is more to it than merely catching fish. . . .*The challenge of bluegills and perch thins with time. *This is easy and anyone can do it*, a boy says to himself. He knows about tackle and other techniques from the magazines, and he is ready to try. It is absolutely inevitable that he will want to catch larger fish and own fine tackle. But there is no sure moral outcome. The possibility of corruption is there. The eager boy may become a bragging, fish-hogging boor who fishes to keep score and prove something. But the other possibility is there, too. He may become a fine fisherman and a man with enough wit to see his sport and even himself for what they are. Salvation lies in keeping part of the boy alive in the maturing man.

John Voelker writes (under the nom de plume Robert Traver) of sitting on the bank of a river as a boy and watching as the man he wanted to become caught a large trout. Voelker, having fished all day with primitive equipment and unpolished technique, was frustrated and impatient, and he had climbed out of the river to rest and think. Maybe it was not going to work out with him and fly-fishing, he thought. Perhaps the ingredients just weren't there. He wasn't doing half as well with tackle as he had done with bait.

He watched the Michigan river flow slowly past. Then a fish rose to something in the pool just below him. As Voelker watched, the fish rose again. He sighed and got up to try again with his hand-me-down steel fly rod and a discarded streamer, which he describes as a "feathered anvil." The fish rose again. A feeding pattern was apparent, and Voelker was about to step into the stream to take advantage of it when he noticed another fisherman, downstream from him, working his way slowly toward the pool where the solitary fish was rising. Voelker climbed back up the bank and chose a spot from which he could watch the stalk unfold.

The fisherman turned out to be an old man who was casting a dry fly with a delicate, whippy cane rod. He made precise casts and worked each one out all the way before lifting the little fly off the water, drying it with a couple of effortless false casts, then sending it out on the water for another float. The old man worked each likely-looking spot with the same measured and deliberate care; his attention

never seemed to waver. Then he looked upstream and saw the rising fish. Instead of passing by the intervening water and going directly upstream to the pool, he turned back to the section of the river where he was standing and fished it carefully and patiently, with no show of haste or urgency.

He came on; casting and following out each cast, false casting to dry the fly, then casting it onto the water again. It was a rhythmic and lulling scene, except for the presence of the fish, which continued to rise in the pool just below the hidden Voelker, who could hardly stand it. That fish was ready; what was the old man waiting for?

As the man came on his deliberate way, Voelker could see that he was truly old—not far from doddering. Voelker was surprised that he could wade at all, much less upstream in the correct dry-fly fashion.

Finally the old man was in range. Voelker could hardly contain his excitement, but the old man was still calm. He inspected his fly and decided to tie on another. He looked through two or three fly boxes before he found the pattern he wanted. He knotted the new fly to his tippet and trimmed the excess gut and hackle. He dressed the fly with a little something to make it float better, and then, when all was ready and everything was back in the proper pocket of his vest, he began false casting and timing the trout's rises. Finally, he shot a perfect cast, and the fly landed three or four feet upstream of the fish on a perfect quartering angle. Voelker held his breath as the little speck of hackle and feather rode downstream on the surface film. He almost shouted when the fish took.

The old man had a time with the fish, which turned out to be a large one. Two or three times he shipped water over the tops of his waders as he changed position to follow the fish. There were several fine runs and splashy attempts to fall back on the leader and break it. But the old man held, and finally he brought the fish in next to his hip and scooped it in his landing net. The fish lay bowed in the fabric sack, too tired to move, as the old man turned his catch from one side to another to admire it. Then he reached down into the net and, with the dainty care of a surgeon, took the hook from the trout's mouth. He picked

the tired fish up with gentle hands and lowered it into the water. He held it for a few seconds while its strength returned and its gills began to take in water again. Then he let the fish go. He inspected his fly for damage, found none, began false casting, and once again made his precarious way upstream, working every bit of likely water. Voelker, still watching from his concealed position, decided that was the man he would grow up to be.

All this happened more years ago than Voelker admits. But the lesson took. When I fished with Voelker at his secret pond in north Michigan, he had become that man . . . and a little more. He is a fishing sage who is known best as the author of *Anatomy of a Murder*, but he probably likes that book less than his two volumes of fishing stories collected under the titles *Trout Madness* and *Trout Magic*. Voelker was a justice of the Michigan Supreme Court, then quit when he could afford to, which was after *Anatomy* became a best-seller. (That may be one way of beating the first great law of fishing—*No fisherman ever fishes as much as he wants to*—but it is far from surefire.) In retirement Voelker fishes and writes about fishing and has a fine time. He may have become that man, but he is still that boy, too.

There is no sin in a boy's catching and keeping more panfish than he needs. The point is to catch fish, after all; and if one fish is good, two must be better. If twenty bluegills make a nice stringer, forty are twice as good. The untutored fishing sensibility wants more and bigger fish. And until a boy has caught some fish and put them on a stringer, he probably will not be satisfied with anything less. A boy raised on catch and release probably cannot see the point. The thrill of the release—and it is a thrill—is something that has to be learned.

In a paradoxical way, sport fishing has kept fish populations healthy. As a boy becomes more serious about fishing, there is less of a threat that he will endanger any

"MATCHING THE HATCH—RAINBOW TROUT"—MARK SUSINNO

species. A big score becomes less important. Something else becomes the end of his fishing. It is elusive and not, sadly, for everyone.

The important thing becomes *doing it right*. It has something to do with style and something to do with manners. A lot of it is sheer technique that can be learned only through instruction and application. When a boy is ready to leave panfish, cane poles, and night crawlers, the hard work begins.

Say he wants to learn how to use a fly rod. He knows through reading and perhaps an experience similar to Voelker's that this is where the path will ultimately take him. Before he can do anything, however, he must learn about the tackle and they way it works. It isn't easy. Listen:

"If you have never picked up a fly rod before, you will soon find it factually and theologically true that man by nature is a damn mess. The four-and-a-half-ounce thing in silk wrappings that trembles with the underskin motions of the flesh becomes a stick without brains, refusing anything simple that is wanted of it. All that a rod has to do is lift the line, the leader, and the fly off the water, give them a good toss over the head, and then shoot them forward so they will land in the water without a splash in the following order: fly, transparent leader, and then the line—otherwise the fish will see the fly is fake and be gone. . . .

"Well until man is redeemed he will always take a fly rod too far back, just as natural man always overswings with an ax or golf club . . . only with a rod it's worse, because the fly often comes so far back it gets caught behind in bush or a rock. . . .

"Then, since it is natural for man to try to attain power without recovering grace, he whips the line back and forth making it whistle each way, and sometimes even snapping off the fly from the leader, but the power that was going to transport the little fly across the river somehow gets diverted into building a bird's nest of line, leader, and fly that falls out of the air into the water about ten feet in front of the fisherman. If, though, he pictures the round trip of the line, transparent leader, and fly from the time they leave the water until they return, they are easier to cast. They naturally come off the water heavy line first and in front, and light transparent leader and fly trailing behind. But as they pass overhead they have to have a little beat of time so the light transparent leader and fly can catch up to the heavy line now starting forward and again fall behind it; otherwise the line starting on its return trip will collide with the leader and fly still on their way up, and the mess will be the bird's nest that splashes into the water ten feet in front of the fisherman."

And so on, until the author, Norman MacLean, remembers his instructor and his wisdom: "My father was very sure about certain matters pertaining to the universe. To him, all good things—trout as well as eternal salvation—come by grace and grace comes by art and art does not come easy."

It is easier—a little—today. The tackle is better and standards are so subjective in fly-fishing—as in almost everything else—that they have virtually ceased to be standards at all. I was taught to cast by keeping a book tucked between my upper arm and my body, so that only the forearm and wrist operated the rod.

Lefty Kreh, top rod among present-day fly casters, uses forearm, upper arm, shoulder, and body in a casting technique that is not so much unorthodox as heretical. The emphasis is on what works for you, in fly-fishing as in too many other things. As long as you can put power to your line and keep a tight loop, you are doing fine. The measure of your ability is whether you can get the fly out where you want it without scaring the fish.

But that is a tall enough order, and whatever system you settle on, it takes practice before you can cast well enough to fish with a fly rod. Many, many boys have spent countless hours practicing on lawns, where things are a little easier without the current of the stream to contend with. Even then it is hard to remember to pause at the top of the cast while the line straightens out behind; to control the slack with the left hand; to keep the rod tip up so that the loop won't collapse on the forward stroke. Clean pickup and shoot the line; over and over again until the vectors smooth and fuse into one dynamic that might look awkward to a bystander but feels fluid and natural to the caster.

But casting is not the end of learning. In fact, it is only the beginning. A boy needs to learn fly patterns. Some boys—those who are good at wood carving and model airplane building—may start tying flies, which almost certainly becomes a lifelong obsession.

Trout fishing calls for stealth and some tactical skills. Wading upstream and casting on a quarter to the river's flow do not come easily and naturally. When you step into running water, you want to walk and cast downstream.

But sound methodology and a snobbish Anglo notion of the way things should be done demand that the dry fly—especially the dry fly—be fished upstream. It does come closer to imitating natural conditions than a downstream drift (though that seems less important in this world than in the old one that has passed forever into history, taking with it pocket watches, straight razors, and gentlemen). Handled properly, the dry fly bounces along the surface of the stream free of drag when it is fished upstream; that is, the action of the water on the line is not apparent in the float of the fly, and there is no telltale wake to alert the fish and put them off their feed. Drag is the sworn and constant enemy of the dry-fly fisherman. A boy learns that the first time he steps into a stream.

The feathery intricacy of trout fishing can daunt some boys. One does not have to be a hardened skeptic to doubt the whole proposition. The small fly does not really look like a mayfly at all, or like anything else that occurs in nature. The fine, fragile leaders don't look strong enough to hold a finger-sized bluegill, let alone a two-pound trout. Casting and wading still seem like dubious methods. Better to stay on the bank or get into a boat, to put something alive on the hook, and leave it in the water until a fish eats it. Once again, the boy has to be convinced that the thing can be done. He needs to catch some fish.

Best, then, to start on a river that has plenty of fish and perhaps has a few stockers mixed with the natives. There will be plenty of time later for a boy to perfect his disdain for hatchery fish and natural bait. When he is young, all trout look the same and he isn't concerned about pedigrees.

Even a good stream with a large population of natives and stockers and no-kill regulations is no sure thing, as any trout fisherman will tell you. The best thing that can happen to a young fisherman, then, is to be on a good stream during a major hatch: the Beaverkill during the shad flies; the Ausable during the Hendricksons; the Madison during the salmon flies. In the face of that kind of evidence, all skepticism vanishes. You can catch fish and you can see plainly why it is that you catch fish. Also, you are a witness to the cycle of life

in its most intense, accelerated form. There is something frenzied and a little mad about it. It makes an impression on a boy, like watching the migration of thousands of geese driven by deep, unknowable instinct.

Another, and in some ways better, time to learn about trout fishing with the fly, and to witness the fact that it can be done, is during the hot middle summer. The streams are low then. They are almost naked, and everything is revealed in water that is clear as it is in no other season. This is the best time to learn how to "fish the water."

Also, in the middle of a hot summer day, you can fish big, visible flies that float high and bright instead of tiny mayfly imitations or the underwater nymphs or wets. When a boy locates a dark, shady cut bank with some over-hanging grass and puts a Joe's Hopper on a no. 10 hook a few feet upstream of it and gets a solid brown for his trouble, he has learned a lot about trout fishing and has a good reason to stay with it. Furthermore, the early-season hatches can occur on cold and windy days when the fingers are too numb to change flies and a pinhole in your waders feels like a frozen ice pick. In the hot summer, standing hip-high in cold running water feels like just the thing.

There are all sorts of occurrences that can persuade a skeptical boy. I know one man who had been dutifully following his father around from stream to stream for most of one season years ago. He had two or three fish, hooked blind on wet Coachmans, for his trouble. It was late August, and he was ready to quit fly-fishing altogether and go back to Dardevles for pike and worms for bluegills.

He and his father were working their way upstream in a swift little brown river that ran through low, swampy country between walls of leafy tag alders. It was hot, so hot that he was steaming inside his rubber waders. Every few minutes he would take off his old cotton hat and dip it into the stream, then put it back on his head. The cool water dripping down his neck gave him some relief.

"MATCHING THE HATCH—BROOK TROUT"–MARK SUSINNO

Cumulus clouds building to the west over Lake Michigan billowed and turned dark blue at the edges. Soon they had risen fully twenty thousand feet and turned the color of a day-old bruise. The air went cool and a breeze came up. The sudden drop of pressure was palpable.

There was some lightning and thunder, and the boy's father signaled for him to leave the river and meet him on the bank. The boy acknowledged and, as he was reeling in, felt the frustration of another day of profitless casting. As he was leaving the stream, he noticed some kind of small gray insect pop off the surface of the water. Then another. As he watched, the numbers multiplied, and soon he was witnessing a genuine hatch of some anonymous, late-season mayflies.

Fish began striking as the air became still, the way it does only in the last few minutes before a storm. The boy hastily tied on a fly, something small and gray. He made a cast to the nearest rising fish, which took the fly so eagerly that the boy thought at first it must be a mistake. Perhaps the fish was coming up and the fly had just drifted into its open mouth. He quickly brought in the brown, the nicest he ever caught, and killed it with the back of a pocketknife. The fish went into the creel that the boy had never before used. He cast to another rising fish, which took with as much energy as the first. He played that one out and put it into the creel with the other, feeling that this one was truly earned. And so it went for ten or fifteen minutes. The lightning flashed into the tall cedars on either side of the river. The thunder rolled ponderously. And the boy fished on, putting his first limit of trout into his creel and taking his chances with the storm,

which he did not notice anyway. The fishing ended when the rain finally collected and came in sheets, drowning the little insects and putting the feeding fish back down. The boy left the river giddy from the fishing and the storm's ozone. "I wouldn't do it again," he told me years later, "stand out in the middle of a river during an electrical storm with a nine-foot lightning rod in my hand. But I wouldn't trade that one time for anything." . . .Most things end naturally, if painfully, for a boy. He realizes he will never throw the ball like Bradshaw or hit like Alou. So he puts his toys away.

Fishing is not something you grow out of, but for some reason most boys walk away from it for a while. Automobiles and girls come along to take their time and attention. Boys grow up enough to make fools of themselves and terrify their parents the way they never did when they were digging for worms and going off to some secret pond to fish.

It is impossible to know why boys lose interest in fishing. It is not biology, because some boys never do. But most do and some, sadly, never come back. But it should be counted one of fishing's best features that you can always come back to it. That cannot be said of baseball and football, model airplanes, summer camp, swimming holes, and young flirty girls. As years pass you can recall those things and feel the ache, but you can never have them again. You can pick up a rod and go fishing, and if you haven't completely buried the boy in you, there will be something of the old sweet feeling of awe left. You can feel it long after baseball cards and catcher's mitts and bicycles have become dead objects. Even then, a fishing rod still has a magic feeling, a life. Fishing keeps us—part of us, anyway—boys forever.

"But it should be counted one of fishing's best features

that you can always come back to it. . . .You can pick up a rod and go fishing,

and if you haven't completely buried the boy in you, there will be something

of the old sweet feeling of awe left."

Excerpted from
THE ULTIMATE FISHING BOOK

GEOLOGY

& TROUT

Robert H. Smith
1984

WE TEND TO THINK of the landscape around us, our visible world, as permanent and indestructible—the "eternal hills" of the poets, so to speak. Actually, what we see are transient landforms, everchanging over eons on a scale unimaginable. Ever since the earth's crust hardened there have been periods of cataclysmic convulsions: shearings, thrustings, foldings and tiltings, with upwellings of magma spouting forth as volcanoes or passive fissure flows, forcing segments of crust along zones of weakness and stress to manifest as mountain ranges, valleys or awesome trenches under the sea.

No sooner had the continental crust been elevated into domes and ridges than the forces of destruction took over. Rain, running water, frost and wind began the slow transport of the detritus to lower levels, the valleys and the sea. Once the crust was base leveled, the sea encroached upon the lowlands and vast deposits of sediment accumulated, finally becoming sedimentary rocks, their tremendous weight triggering further adjustments of the crust and starting

the process all over again—the new building on the stumps of the old.

These planetary paroxysms appear to occur in ordered sequence, the slow "rhythm of geological time," separated by a quarter billion years with intervening periods of minor uplifts, each followed by a glacial period. There have been at least four of these major mountain forming epochs and we live near the close of the last one, when the uplands are still high, carved into jagged crests and peaks by glacial ice. In fact, the last glaciation is still manifest; there is enough water locked up in present land ice to raise the sea level two hundred feet or more, should it all melt.

Moreover, the crust is still shifting about as molten magma deep within the earth upwells in convection currents, jostling tectonic plates against each other, causing tremors and vulcanism. In the Cascade Mountain Range in Washington State, the eruption in 1980 of Mount St. Helens blew 1300 feet off her peak in response to such internal pressures, scattering volcanic debris far and wide in a cataclysmic explosion that devastated forest

lands, obliterated lakes and laid waste over 150 miles of prime trout and salmon streams. St. Helens has done this several times in the past, her last previous eruption occurring in 1842. Yet after each holocaust the surrounding streams purged themselves of ash and mud flows and the trout and salmon populations reestablished themselves.

There are hundreds of other volcanoes in the "ring of fire" girdling the Pacific, some believed to be "extinct," others quite active and still smoldering, biding time until pressures build up to force eruptions. Those of us who live in the Pacific Northwest dwell in their shadows as witnesses to what has happened in the past and predictors of what is likely to occur in the future.

Even though our time coincides with the close of the last great epoch of uplift and distortion, there are still adjustments being made as continental blocks seek to attain equilibrium with surrounding masses and the up-welling of molten magma from the depths continues to drag the tectonic plates around

like pans of shifting pack ice in the Arctic Sea.

If it were not for the mountains extending high up into the heavens, the planetary winds would circle the globe unobstructed and the weather would not be worthy of discussion. The climate would be uniform, monotonous, varying only with latitude and whether oceanic or continental. But the mountain barriers have changed all that, diverting the even flow of air, causing eddies and cross currents, forcing it upward, cooling it and causing condensation of water vapor to fall as rain or snow. Thus we owe

our present diversification of climates to the past convulsions of the earth's crust, which has made possible the multitude of microclimates and ecological niches found in mountainous regions; where we may find a rain forest on one side of a range and a desert on the other.

The aggregate impact of these past events has shaped the destinies of all living things. Some, unable to adapt to the vast changes, became extinct. Others, more suited to survive the changes in the environment, prospered and evolved into new genera and species. The

"FLY FISHING—JACKSON HOLE"–JOSEPH SULKOWSKI

process continues. Since these slow changes do not seem to account for the mass extinctions such as befell the dinosaurs and mammoths, it is theorized that other cataclysmic events as yet undetermined must have occurred.

Of all evolving living creatures, the fishes of the sea were the least affected by the geological events that were altering the face of the globe. The oceans respond more slowly and to a lesser degree to climatic changes wrought by crustal upheavals and provide a much more equitable environment for marine life than the often harsh conditions the continents offered to land-based creatures. Consequently, evolutionary changes in sea creatures have been slower and less dramatic than in land animals and as a result there are still many primitive types of fish in existence today. One such fish, a "living fossil," was hauled up off the African coast in 1938 and christened *Latimeria*, a member of the Coelacanths which were thought to have been extinct since the Cretaceous Period 60 to 100 million years ago, a time when dinosaurs still trod upon the earth.

93

The salmonids are also a primitive type of fish in form and structure with earliest known fossil records going back 40 to 60 million years ago to the Eocene Epoch. As cold water adapted fish, trout and salmon probably evolved in the Arctic, possibly 10 million years ago, when the climate of that region resembled that of our temperate zone today. Shortly thereafter the ancestors of the European brown trout and Atlantic salmon may have become isolated from the ancestors of the trout and salmon of the North Pacific region. It is thought that North America was the place of origin of these western trout and salmon and that they became established in Eastern Asia by way of the Bering Land Bridge which appeared at intervals during the last glacial epoch.

Before vulcanism built up the Cascade Range and well before the last glaciation, a giant saber-toothed salmon and a trout called *Rhabdofario* found a home in what are now the desert basins of Eastern Oregon, leaving their fossils buried in sediment. Although *Rhabdofario* became the common trout of Western North America during the Pliocene Epoch immediately preceding the last glacial period, it is not known exactly when or from what ancestors our modern trout evolved.

Probably the first of the present races of trout to become established on the Pacific Slope was the Mexican golden trout, the probable progenitor of the Apache and the Gila trout. The Mexican golden trout may also have been a remote ancestor of the redbands and the rainbows which later displaced it except in a few headwaters draining out the Sierra Madre.

The first modern trout to invade the waters of the Pacific Northwest, however, was the cutthroat, and it became established in waters denied latecomers by the formation of impassable barriers. Next on the scene in the Northwest were the redbands, which displaced the cutthroats of interior drainages below the barriers in most places. Finally the rainbows appeared and displaced the redbands where they came in contact.

Thus the geological upheavals of the past built vast mountain ranges, leveled the plains, rearranged the drainage patterns and altered the climate which in turn was responsible for the glaciation that sculptured the high country and accelerated the tearing down processes. All of these actions and interactions have merged to create the myriad ecological niches that now exist, each with its own distinctive plant and animal communities. These are particularly abundant and varied in Western North America resulting in the richest trout fauna in the world. Here they occur throughout five separate life zones—from upper Sonoran to Arctic-Alpine. There are at least five and possibly six recognized species of trout and twenty subspecies, as well as five species of charr each evolved to its present state of adaptation by responses to particular environmental pressures.

What remains today as a legacy to that once abundant and widespread pristine world of trout—particularly in interior drainages—are scattered remnants hanging on precariously in a few remote headwater streams. In roughly

100 years man has practically destroyed that which took natural processes millions of years to create. The degradation of the waters by poor forest practices, overgrazing, channel blocking dams, water diversion and pollution have all contributed to the decimation of native trout populations, but the crowning indignity, the coup de grace, was the introduction of non-native trout resulting in the displacement of natives either through competition or hybridization. It is now a common experience to fish a beautiful mountain stream and catch almost every kind of trout under the sun—except a native! Some anglers and fisheries officials do not seem concerned about this as long as there is plenty of trout to be caught . . . any kind of trout. It is for those of us who do care, who value quality over quantity and hope for the return of the "native" that I have written this book.

Excerpted from
NATIVE TROUT OF NORTH AMERICA

"LATE HOUR ON THE FIREHOLE"–ADRIANO MANOCCHIA

"O for the rush of our darling stream,

With its strips of virgin meadow,

For the morning beam and the evening gleam

Through the deep forest shadow . . ."

SAPTOGUS

Izaak Walton
1653

O for the rush of our darling stream,
　　With its strips of virgin meadow,
For the morning beam and the evening gleam
　　Through the deep forest shadow;
For our dove-like tent, with white wings bent
　　To shield us from the weather,
Where we make our bed of hemlock spread,
　　And sleep in peace together.

O for the free and sinless wild,
　　Far from the city's pother,
Where the spirit mild of Nature's child,
　　On the breast of his holy mother,
In the silence sweet, may hear the beat
　　Of her loving heart and tender,
Nor wish to change the greenwood range
　　For worldly pomp and splendor.

O for the laugh of the merry loon,
　　For the chant of the fearless thrushes,
Who pipe their tune to sun and moon,
　　In clear and liquid gushes;
For the roar of flood, and the echoing wood,
　　And the whisperings above us,
Of the twilight breeze through the trembling trees,
　　Like words of those that love us.

O for a breath of the fresh, pure air,
　　With the smell of the pine and cedar,
And the relish rare, for his simple fare,
　　It gives to the happy feeder;
For the social smoke and the hurtless joke,
　　The snatch of song and chorus,
Ere we tread the slope in cheery hope
　　Of the busy sport before us.

O for the cast, with shrilly whisht,
　　Of golden wing and hackle—
The ready twist of the thrilling wrist—
　　The strain of rod and tackle;
The gallant play of the silvery prey,
　　Reel spinning as they ask it,
And the angler's pride when by his side
　　They fill the ample basket.

O that the willow's leaf were free,
　　And the dogwood were in flower,
When the heart-bound three once more might be
　　Within thy forest bower;
We three, who know where'er we go
　　All other sports are bogus,
Compared with those thy haunts disclose,
　　Thy secret haunts, Saptogus.

from the book
THE COMPLEAT ANGLER

"ROYAL WULFF"—ROCK NEWCOMB

"We take pride now in being non-preying predators and releasing our fish;

but we cannot release a fish until we have captured it so we are still as much

predators as ever whether we keep our fish or put them back. To be a good angler

one must be a good predator."

THE TROUT'S

WORLD

Lee Wulff
1986

WE LIVE in a world of predators and prey; Man has been the fiercest predator of all. When we fish for trout, a predatory act in which we seek to capture a living animal, we are allied with the hawks that prey on the pigeons, we are one with the wolves that take the caribou and the lion that stalks the gazelle. We take pride now in being non-preying predators and releasing our fish; but we cannot release a fish until we have captured it so we are still as much predators as ever whether we keep our fish or put them back. To be a good angler one must be a good predator.

The best fishermen are born to it. The great musicians are born with the gift. So are the great anglers. Intelligent people without the gift can learn the techniques and attain considerable proficiency in either music or angling but they will never be able to go as far as those born with the inherent understanding.

To learn to be a good predator one must study predators whether they be cats or hawks or very successful fisherman. When I watch Ed Van Put, one of the best trout fisherman I know, cast his fly I am reminded of a cat stalking a bird; in him I see the same intentness on his quarry that one does not see in the casual fly fisherman. I know that in his mind there is a picture of the water he fishes over that is not limited to the surface he can see but the flowing liquid beneath it and the imagined trout he is trying to catch as they lie in or move through their life medium. They may or may not be there—but they are likely to be where he has learned they should be and they are likely to respond to the flies he has had them respond to before.

I hope you will develop a similar sense of the flowing waters and the trout's positions in them; I hope you, like Ed, will become one with the real world of nature, the world of predators and prey and the ever-changing balance that is part of their lives.

Man was a hunter for most of his time on earth. It was only six thousand years ago that he became a farmer, which let him cease to be a nomad and settle into cities since he could then store food instead of having to capture or find it anew for each set of hunger pangs. We have only been industrial for less than two hundred years, which further expanded our ability or need to live in cities and further divorced us from living in and with and understanding the natural world. And what does this have to do with trout fishing?

Because of our changed situation, we have changed our society to adapt to our agrarian, industrial system. To understand wild things and how they live we must unlearn some of the basic tenets of our human society. Humans say, "Save the children first." This is natural for us and beneficial to our society. Nature says the opposite. When there is a cold winter with lots of heavy snow, which are the deer that die first? They are the fawns and the smaller deer that are weaker and cannot browse as high as the big bucks and larger does; and so they die of starvation. Nature's premise is that fawns would not be bearing more young the following spring and that the stronger does will, and that the herd will bounce back faster; nature supports the progeny of the best and strongest breeding stock.

Nature is not sentimental. Most city folk are loathe to accept the fact that every living thing will die and most things die violently, by predation and starvation and not old age. The wild world is a wonderful world. Man may consider it cruel but it is fair. It is a world of predators and prey. We have learned not to hate hawks because, in Nature's plan, they are one of the killers like wolves and lions and leopards. It is as much a part of our heritage as it is that of the grizzly. Man may have originated as a vegetarian, but he became the fiercest predator of all, with the power to control all the other animals and build the civilizations we have now.

One may ask, "Which is the superior or higher form of life, the hawk or the dove?" This is a question about nature, not about the Vietnam War. And the answer is that the predator is essentially superior to the prey. It must outfly, outrun, or out-think the living prey it feeds on. The balancing factor that Nature gives to the prey is love—the prey can breed faster. Predators have a lower birth rate and must spend more time training their young to be swifter than their prey and as deadly as possible.

Arthur Godfrey used to say that Man was the only animal who killed for pleasure. He had never seen a fox in a hen house, I guess, and had the fox kill every hen in it not for food but for fun.

He felt animals killed only what they needed. But lions don't eat everything they kill; they leave a great deal for the scavengers that follow them. Predators kill for practice and want to be as good as they can be at the skills that keep them alive. Instinctively they know that some day life will be severe and the best of the breed, the ablest killers, will survive and the less capable will die.

Why do I include this lesson on nature in a trout-fishing book? Lions and foxes are a long way from trout! It is because you should shake yourself free from human thinking if you're going to be able to evaluate the actions of a fish like the trout accurately.

Let us now consider the trout. He is a mid-range predator. Half the time he is scaring minnows and insects to death and the other half he is scared to death by bigger fish, and by fish hawks, fierce eels, otters, mink, and the like. Of course, no animal can truly be scared to death, even half of the time, and not go off the deep end. So trout, like other forms of prey, find zones of safety in which they can relax. This is very important to the trout fisherman. A trout, to be catchable, must be relaxed and predatory,

"CUTTHROAT TROUT"
–ALAN JAMES ROBINSON

not scared. A good trout fisherman should know what scares a trout and makes it uneasy and what circumstances will let it relax and think about food rather than safety.

It may be well at this point to note the trout's three primary needs: safety, food, and comfort. His first consideration is not to be killed. His second is to get enough food to stay alive and hopefully enough to be very happy. A trout also wants to be comfortable—for discomfort is troubling and extreme discomfort, such as water too warm for him to function in, will kill him. A fourth factor, sex, will affect his

activities but with fish that is occasional and has be be considered only on spawning runs.

To understand the trout we must first realize that he is relatively low on the scale of intelligence. He is not as bright as your two-year-old or your Labrador. He is low on the order of brainpower. That doesn't mean he cannot think. He can. Like the old saying, "Once bitten, twice shy," he can learn from experience. But too many people give him credit for knowing what humans know or for thinking like a human. No trout has ever seen a steel mill or knows a hook as a hook unless it has been caught on hooks with their distinctive shape a least a few times. No trout knows that a leader is a leader. He may recognize it as something unnatural attached to what would otherwise seem to be an edible fly—but he does not know very much.

Trout live on their past—like spiders and beavers and weaver birds. Can you spin a spider's web? It would take quite a bit of engineering for a human to create something so delicate and so efficient. Yet a spider with a brain smaller than a bit of dust can do it. If you take a pair of beavers and put them in a closed-in swimming pool and feed them for three generations then turn one of the kits loose the first thing it will do in the wild is build a dam. How much training would it take you to build a dam as efficiently as a beaver with only sticks and mud. Take a pair of weaver birds and keep them in an aviary with only the food they need and send the third generation out into the wild and they will build a nest and use the same special knots their great-grandparents used, never having seen it before or been taught in any manner to make that special knot.

Animals like the trout and the beaver live on the inherited skills of their for bears, what we call instinct. To understand trout you must understand their instinctive reactions. That can be learned through observation. Back in 1947, while flying home from Newfoundland in a Piper Cub, I passed over the tuna-fishing grounds off Wedgeport where I'd caught tuna and been a part of that early fishery. I saw the sport fishing boats beneath me, trolling baits. I knew some of the boats and captains and swung low over them to wave although I knew they wouldn't know who was in the plane. Then I saw three big tuna swimming at the surface and circled to have a good look at them. Accidentally, the shadow of my plane crossed them and with a great splash of water they disappeared into the depths.

No bird is big enough to pick up a quarter-ton tuna and fly away with it yet those fish were scared to death. Maybe when they were tiny a diving bird could have eaten them; but they'd grown to a size where they need have a fear of birds no longer. Still, the fear of something flying was still with them as strongly as ever. Instincts like that are a part of survival. The fish with such instincts have a better survival rate than those that do not. Lower animals survive on many such things embedded in their consciousness. These instincts, which sometimes save them, can be used to capture them as well.

Prior to that incident with the tuna I had been exploring Newfoundland's salmon rivers, estimating their fishing potential and writing about the region's great fishing. I would hike in to a remote stream, camp there and fish; I judged by the fish I could catch in a given time and those I saw and the prevalence of young salmon what the river's potential was. After scaring the tuna I simply waited for a sunny day when the river was running clear and would fly up over the pools of an unknown river at about 250 feet and throw the shadow of my plane on the pool below. Every salmon in the pool would move in fright and I could tell in a minute or two over a pool what had taken many days and miles of hiking before.

Instincts, once established, are slow to fade. In Newfoundland, when I first went down there in the early thirties, there were many harbor seals that swam up into the river to feed on the big trout and the salmon. As a result, I believe, most of the big trout and the salmon used to ease in along shore to the shallow water during the night hours in order to make it more difficult for the seals to surprise them. These seals were a host to a worm that infested the codfish of that area so a bounty was put on the seals and they were swiftly eliminated from the sea and streams. Yet the big trout and salmon will continue to ease in against the shore at night for centuries just as big tuna will still dive from a shadow moving over the sea. It is worthwhile to learn the unthinking weaknesses and strengths of the trout you fish for.

We are still studying nature and have not yet started to fish. And there is more. Trout fishing was a challenging sport when catching other types of fish was simple. The challenge came because the trout's food was made up largely of aquatic insects, many so small that imitating them was a difficult and intriguing problem. The magic in a trout stream lies

"MATCHING THE HATCH—CUTTHROAT TROUT"–MARK SUSINNO

partly in the insects within it. Some are able to change from a living, swimming submarine to a living, flying airplane in a matter of seconds. Some come to the top of the water and, bursting through the surface, fly away. Some drift on the surface just long enough to shed their wet suits and fly off in their pilot's garb. Some crawl out on stones to break out of their underwater clothing and into flying gear that will let them go where the trout can't get at them. All must come back to the water to lay their eggs, usually just dapping down on the surface for the briefest touch-and-go without giving a hungry trout a fair chance to get them.

These aquatic insects have been identified and cataloged and many studious anglers know the Latin names they go by. But trout do not know these names. They know the bugs and they know which ones they like and that is what a good trout fisherman wants to know. The need to know the Latin names is only for identification when talking to another angler so that each may understand the other. Being an artist I can draw or describe any insect I find on a trout stream and so have been slow to learn the Latin names.

Aquatic insects will be covered in the chapter on entomology, and we will move on to study the nature of the trout in his feeding. Trout eat living things, not grasses as carp and suckers do. Anything that moves is fair game and the scope of their feeding is as wide as the sky. As a tiny trout starts to feed he takes into his mouth everything that comes along small enough to get into it; and sometimes, he will take in things he can only swallow if he chews them apart. A fish has no hands and can only examine anything by taking it into his mouth. This is a point to remember: a curious trout will take into his mouth for an instant something he wants to investigate, something he may have only the slightest feeling he'll want to eat or hope will be worth eating.

The growing trout soon learns that most things that drift freely with the current, like bits of wood and leaf and other debris, have no nutritional value; he learns to let them drift on by, saving his energy for what will nourish him. A trout must get enough food to make up for the energy he expends in getting it. But a good predator will have an extra supply of energy for emergencies and to spend, sometimes, out of the pure joy of living or in practice to build strengths and skills against the competition or hard times to come. This trait will be developed later when we study where trout lie in order to minimize the effort required to get their food.

"SPRINGS WIGGLER"–ROCK NEWCOMB

Many of us who fish for brook trout have been lucky enough to see one come out of the water in a clean leap and, descending head first, take our fly on his return to the water instead of coming up to get it from below. What we have seen is sheer exuberance, and pride in a skillful maneuver. I have seen the same thing with a rare salmon. Why does it happen? Is it showing off because in earlier feeding the fish has gained so much energy for the effort he's put into it that he has energy to spare? Is it to show off for his own satisfaction or for another trout that might be there to see? Fish are keenly aware of other fish. And they are highly competitive. If I get a particularly savage strike at my fly my first thought is that

there may be another (or other) trout close by and my trout raced to get there first.

Curiosity and jealousy are both present. How many times have I seen one trout follow another that was hooked until my presence was definitely determined as dangerous? It was probably because the following fish thought the hooked one had a morsel too big to handle and that he, the second fish, might muscle in and get a share. This happens often with bass. A bass hooked on a plug that stays outside the fish's mouth will be followed by another who will strike at the plug to take it away, occasionally being hooked and landed, both fish attached to the same multiple-hooked lure. This competitiveness is true with trout. It is true with bass. It is true with seagulls and with practically all predators.

Feeding the trout in our ponds one sees their competition and jealousy. When I throw out a handful of pellets they rush swiftly to get those they can see before the other fish do. However, if I throw pellets in one at a time when they're hungry they'll rush for them at top speed to get there ahead of the other trout. Often they'll bump one another hard as they make contact at the pellet. On one occasion two trout came to the pellet from opposite directions and the twelve incher's head drove right into the mouth of the eighteen incher coming the other way.

The trout learns that the things that move, either through the water or within themselves (like the pulsating of a mayfly's gills or the swimming motion of a nymph's legs or body) are living and edible. Motion becomes his first and major criterion as to whether something he sees is edible and worth chasing or not. Motion, either of or within a fly, has caught more trout than anything else.

To understand this better it is important to realize that for the first four centuries of fly fishing only wet flies were used. Wet flies are built with *wings* and a body, hackle (legs) and tail. Trout rarely if ever expected to see a *winged* insect moving *under the water* and no winged, flying insect ever wanted to be there. Yet in those early centuries thousands of trout were caught on wet flies and the early British anglers scoured the world for the fanciest of feathers to make them beautiful. When fly fisherman finally realized that winged flies *under water*—

with few exceptions—were unnatural, they began to shift to imitations of the underwater forms of the aquatic insects, the nymphs; then hundreds and hundreds of the early wet-fly patterns many anglers felt they could not do without drifted off into oblivion. How many of today's fly fisherman could describe or recognize a Greenwell's Glory, a Wickham's Fancy, or an Alexandra, the latter a fly that, stories go, was so deadly it was barred on many British streams?

Even today as many or more trout are caught on flies no trout ever dreamed of seeing than on imitations of the old standbys they feed on. The trout, a tough competitor in his class, sees something drifting along toward him. He's never seen anything like it. But it moves and must be alive. He grabs it before some other trout can get to it. Maybe it is a beetle that rarely or never gets to a stream. It might be a praying mantis, the first insect of its kind in that stream's valley, or a Mickey Finn, a streamer fly of red and yellow and silver, that looks like nothing he has ever seen before.

Picture the trout lying in his selected feeding spot. A few hunger pangs heighten his awareness of things around him. He's strong and feisty on this late spring day. Along comes something swimming or drifting across his vision. He's old enough and wise enough to have a little caution, having been hooked and escaped a time or two; but this thing is intriguing. It has colors in a combination never seen before. It swims in a way that's most unusual. He studies it and realizes that this is something truly different.

"SULFER HATCH—BROWN TROUT"–MARK SUSINNO

But what is it?

Is it good to eat?

What will it taste like?

It's moving out of range and it's now or never. If he lets it go by he'll never know what it would taste like and he decides to find out. They say curiosity kills cats; the same holds true for trout.

Trout will hide and when they have hidden you cannot catch them on a fly. I have waded across the Beaverkill and, stepping on a flat-topped stone, sent a good trout scurrying out from under it to safer water somewhere else. Trout will ease in under overhanging banks and nestle in hiding against the earth or roots or weed growth. On a caribou-hunting trip our luck was poor at first and, in order to get some trout to vary our diet from bacon and beans, I "tiggled" some trout. I would walk along the edge of the stream until I saw a fish dart under a bank. Then, quietly, I would slowly feel around with my hand until I found the trout. A gentle stroking on their flesh seems to soothe rather than bother them. When the exact position of the fish is determined a quick closing of the hand can provide a grip that will hold them. "Tiggling" is an old poacher's method that requires no complex tackle, just understanding and skill.

It is easy to see that there is a great deal to learn about the trout and his ways. We have made a beginning. Studying the ways of trout can be a lifelong interest, with new and surprising insights possible for even the wisest of old-time anglers.

The diurnal temperature change may be as much as 20° or more between the cool of dawn and the heat of the four o'clock peak in the afternoon. Checking the temperatures at enough times on enough days will give you a good sense of these daily temperature patterns—and this can help with your fishing. You'll know then that if the temperature on a given day is 70° at four o'clock it will drop at a rate of 3° an hour on that kind of day and that by six you should have a decent chance for some of good fishing.

When the trout streams get up around 80°, trout start dying. Our conservation laws have not yet caught up with what is a very serious problem for trout. When the trout, to stay alive, must gather in small tributaries or, more often, in great schools of hundreds in the cooler water of big rivers at the mouths of the tributaries, they are in great danger. If an angler hooks and plays them, no matter how carefully, they're likely to die from the exertion. When these trout are in concentrated waters where they may be caught and *kept*, word goes out and often hundreds are taken easily—that would provide quite a challenge at any other time.

It is hard to understand why the streams are not closed to all fishing at such times. Woods are closed because of fire hazards. Why can't the trout streams be closed to fisherman when catching fish at such time is such a threat to future fishing in those rivers? By permitting fishing at such times we are losing the best wild breeding stock we have.

Knowledge of water temperatures and their effect on the behavior of our quarry can thus be of great help to us as we pursue trout—and it can also help us preserve our fisheries.

→ Trout Vision

Can trout see color? The scientists tell us they can. Do they see color as we do? Ah! That's another question.

We know that bees, like trout, have eyes that give them the capacity to see color. But we've found that bees, although they see color, do not see color as we do. They utilize a different segment of the color scale and just as a dog can hear a whistle that is above our sound range, bees can see colors that we can't. A flower that looks plain white to us can have a set of arrows on the petals pointing as if to say to the bees, "Here's the nectar. Come and get it."

Think for a moment. The chance that trout see color exactly as we do, I believe, is extremely slim. And what does that do to all the color-concentrating fly fisherman and fly tyers? It should shake them a little. If we found out that trout could not see color at all that would really drive us bonkers.

I go under the assumption that trout can see color and use it for identification just as humans do. I'm certain they see it differently than I do, perhaps like a color-blind human, and I am able to live with that. I just hope that my versions of flies in color patterns satisfying to me satisfy them, too, in their own, different way. How important color is in the flies we use is likely to remain a subject of conjecture for a long, long time. I knew an angler who made all his flies in black or white or shades of gray because he believed color didn't matter—and he caught a lot of trout. Color was off the bottom of the chart on his list of matters of

"STREAMER"–ROCK NEWCOMB

importance to trout. It's pretty well down on mine, too. Yet I love to make beautiful flies and, as mentioned above, I hope that my flies intrigue the trout no matter through what spectrum they view them.

Flies are works of art. I tie mine as much for my own pleasure in the choice of colors as for the particular effectiveness of those colors. I concentrate on the light and dark aspects for effectiveness. The speckled aspect of an Adams looks buggy to me. The stark color breaks of Mickey Finn have a special character, regardless of color. The dark back and light underside of a stonefly nymph or a minnow has to be important to a trout. Reverse it and the insect or minnow is swimming upside down.

The size and shape of a fly are, I believe, far more important than the color—although I can imagine a situation where the color or color pattern might be the deciding factor for a trout in whether or not to take a fly of a satis-

factory shape and size. It is harder to determine, though, whether size and shape is the most important. No doubt both are extremely important when trying to match a hatch. In a sense each is a part of the other. If the shape of the nymph is that of a stonefly, how much will it matter to a trout if the fly is small or large and he's hungry? In the case of the sculpin or darter, the shape is the definitive thing. If the trout are rising to little roundish beetles or midge pupae, then the size will probably be the most important factor in a feeding trout's decision. To be really successful, the trout fisherman must consider all factors and make his choices on the basis of whether or not the finished fly will do the job.

A trout's ability to see and recognize colors as we see them is one thing; knowing *what* he can see is another—and a more important—matter. Because he lives in water and must look through it and sometimes on into the air beyond where the surface bends the light waves, his vision has to be distorted just as a human vision of things seen underwater at an angle is distorted. The difference between the angle of incidence and the angle of refraction, which is the "bend" or change in direction of the vision in water, maximizes at about 49°. An angler standing on the shore and looking at a fish a few feet underwater will have the illusion that the fish is farther away than he really is; this is because of the bending of the light waves, a bending that varies with the varying of the angler's vision from vertical where there's zero bend.

Water not only refracts light but also reflects it. Therein lies a problem for humans trying to determine just what a trout can or cannot see. I smile every time I see one of the familiar illustrations showing a trout's "cone of vision" as determined by a scientist. I smile because they are always shown in absolutely still water, with the trout looking up through a perfect circle. This is pretty silly because where, in trout streams, do we have *perfectly flat* water? Put your eye down near the surface to glance along it and you'll see lifts and drops where it moves, even very slowly, over obstacles on the streambed. Look for the ripples of wind.

To base a premise on what trout can see under such perfectly still-water conditions doesn't make sense. The moment the water moves at all the whole idea that a trout can only see out of this little perfect circle becomes untenable. The bending water bends the light waves in all directions and at some point in some wave a trout can see through the water surface to everything above it in the sky or on shore.

None of these technical articles I read end up with a field test to prove their conclusions. They don't use a very directional strobe light and flash it to make sure there is no effect on a trout in an area where they've determined he can't see. Small boys, sneaking up on trout in small streams, are careful to keep hidden because they've learned a simple truth: that if you can see a trout, he can see you—and that you can see him even though you're not looking into the water through his cone of vision.

Looking through waves that come in quick succession, especially small ripples, will give momentary images that come and go with the waves like our moving pictures (which consist of twenty-four still images per second and which our eye translates into continuous motion). Great physical capabilities are developed when they become a life or death matter. It is important for a trout to see and recognize danger. Their seeing may be developed to a degree it is hard for us to understand.

There's no question but that a trout gets reflection from the undersurface of the water and that this can and does interfere with his clear vision; but there's also no question but that you, if you make your own tests, will find that they can see motions and signs of danger through a very wide range. Unless they're backed up by field tests, it's wise to figure that a trout doesn't have too many blind spots.

Excerpted from
TROUT ON A FLY

ANATOMY

of a FISHERMAN

Robert Traver
1964

⇸ Testament of a Fisherman

I fish because I love to; because I love the environs where trout are found, which are invariably beautiful, and hate the environs where crowds of people are found, which are invariably ugly; because of all the television commercials, cocktail parties, and assorted social posturing I thus escape; because, in a world where most men seem to spend their lives doing things they hate, my fishing is at once an endless source of delight and an act of small rebellion; because trout do not lie or cheat and cannot be bought or bribed or impressed by power, but respond only to quietude and humility and endless patience; because I suspect that men are going along this way for the last time, and I for one don't want to waste the trip; because mercifully there are no telephones on trout waters; because only in the woods can I find solitude without loneliness; because bourbon out of an old tin cup always tastes better out there; because maybe one day I will catch a mermaid; and, finally, not because I regard fishing as being so terribly important but because I suspect that so many of the other concerns of men are equally unimportant—and not nearly so much fun.

⇸ On Trout Fishing and the Sturdy Virtues

Old fisherman never die; instead they write books about their passion, usually couched in a mournful, elegiac, Thoreauesque prose—withal larded with a sort of dogged jocularity—that old fishermen seem helplessly bound to employ when they put down rod and take up pen and look back on all the trout they slew. "Trouting on the Old Nostalgia" might serve as the collective title of most of these wistful memoirs, some of which are best read to the throbbing accompaniment of an old movie Wurlitzer. Worst of all, too many of these books feed the myth that trout fishing promotes health, serenity and frugality in its disciplines.

This is a lot of pious nonsense. Chasing trout is no less wearing and barely less complicated than chasing women. And more frustrating, too, because women, I have heard, are rather more readily overtaken and caught. As for the frugality bit, I swear my trout run me five dollars an ounce. Troy weight.

The truth is that trout fisherman scheme and lie and toss in their sleep. They dream of great dripping trout, shapely and elusive as mermaids, and arise cranky and haggard from their fantasies. They are moody and neglectful and all of them a little daft. Moreover they are inclined to drink too much.

The truth is that fishing for trout is as crazy and self-indulgent as inhaling opium. What, then, can be said for trout fishing? Simply this: it's got work beat a mile and is, if a man can stand it, indecently great fun.

→ Are All Fishermen Alike?

No, thank heaven. Fishermen vary as violently as do other men, and in their fishing they are just as apt to reveal their individual tastes and phobias and basic drives. For among fishermen, as in the stock market, there are the bulls and bears, the plungers and the timid souls, the lambs and the foxes, the avid ones and the dreamy fugitives from Walden. And each of us reveals it in his fishing. Perhaps it all boils down to just what men look for in their fishing.

Thus some fishermen seek only to catch enormous fish in far places where they must cast from here to eternity. Talking a mysterious professional patter, bristling with rod cases and passports, their fishing trips tend to be as big a deal as society weddings or African safaris. We can see their pictures monthly in the outdoor magazines, one big fish holding aloft another, the two being distinguished largely by a triumphant grin. These are the jolly "kill-kill" boys among fishermen, the tanned hearty lads who I am at pains to avoid, and for whom I suspect the outdoors is but a suburb of their egos.

At the opposite extreme are the quiet anonymous fishermen who cling wistfully to their amateur standing, whose pictures rarely adorn the outdoor magazines, and who are quite content to seek more modest trout on fine tackle, perhaps on the comforting theory that it may take as much if not more subtlety and skill to fool their own heavily fished native trout than to engage a spotted whale on some virginal torrent in the Argentine. Perhaps this is only one man's small rebellion against this whole tedious bigger-and-better philosophy as it more and more afflicts our outdoors, indeed our very life. Perhaps it is pure envy. In any case, those easy uncluttered fisherman who do not weigh and calibrate their pleasure are the guys I like to fish with.

Possibly the most revealing difference between these two types of fishermen is what each does with his fish. The quiet fisherman either returns or eats the trout he catches; the kill-kill boys—after photographs, of course— invariably clap theirs on the wall. There are times when I yearn to reunite them there.

Excerpted from
ANATOMY OF A FISHERMAN

"A FINE CATCH"–JOSEPH SULKOWSKI

TROUT

MADNESS

Robert Traver
1984

⇥ The First Day

The true fisherman approaches the first day of fishing with all the sense of wonder and awe of a child approaching Christmas. There is the same ecstatic counting of the days; the same eager and palpitant preparations; the same loving drafting of lists which are succeeded in turn by lists of lists! And then—when time seems frozen in its tracks and one is sure the magic hour will never arrive—lo, *'tis the night before fishing!* Tomorrow is the big day! Perhaps it is also the time for a little poetry, however bad . . .

> *'Twas the night before fishing*
> *When all through the house*
> *Lay Dad's scattered fishing gear*
> *As though strewn by a souse . . .*

Dad will of course have been up a dozen times during the night, prowling the midnight halls, peering out at glowering skies, creeping downstairs and pawing through mounds of duffel for the umpteenth last-minute checkup, crouching over the radio listening to the bright chatter of the all-night disk jockeys, ritualistically tapping the barometer—and perhaps even tapping his medicinal bottle of Kentucky chillchaser. . . . It is this boyish quality of innocence, this irrepressible sense of anticipation, that makes all children and fishermen one. For after all, aren't fishermen merely permanently spellbound juveniles who have traded in Santa Claus for Izaak Walton?

Just as no Christmas can ever quite disappoint a youngster, however bleak and stormy the day, so no opening day of fishing can ever quite disappoint his grown-up brother. The day is invested with its own special magic, a magic that nothing can dispel. It is the signal for the end of the long winter hibernation, the widening of prison doors, the symbol of one of nature's greatest miracles, the annual unlocking of spring.

Since this fisherman dwells at Latitude 45 it should come as no great shock to learn that on most opening days I am obliged to draw rather heavily on this supply of magic to keep up my own drooping spirits. It is sometimes difficult to remain spellbound while mired to the hub caps in mud. *Our* big opening-day problem is twofold: to know where to find ice-free open water; and then be able to get there. During the ordeal we are sometimes driven to drink.

Our opening day is the last Saturday in April, ordinarily a disenchanting season of the year that finds most back roads badly clogged if not impassable, and a four-pound ice chisel a more promising weapon with which to probe our trout waters than a four-ounce fly rod. Our lakes and ponds are usually still ice-locked; our rivers and streams are usually in their fullest flood; and the most sensible solution is to try to remember a partially open spring-fed pond or beaver dam—and then spend a good part of the day trying to get there. Hence it is that my fishing pals and I usually take several pre-season reconnaissance trips on snowshoes. But regardless of the day, always we bravely go forth, come fire, flood, or famine—or the fulminations of relatives by marriage.

On many opening days I have had to trek into the chosen spot on snowshoes. I remember one recent spring when I stood on the foot-thick ice of a pond on my snowshoes—and took eight respectable trout on dry flies from a small open spring-hole less than thirty feet away, skidding them home to daddy over the ice! If you don't believe it, don't let it bother you; I'm not quite sure I believe it myself.

Since 1936 I have kept a complete record of every fishing trip I have taken. It is amazing how I can torture myself during the winter reading over this stuff, recreating once again those magic scenes, seeing again the soft velvet glitter of trout waters, hearing once again the slow rhythmic whish of the fly lines. . . . From those records one thing emerges rather clearly: past opening days were more apt to lean to the mildly tragic than magic. Here is the actual depressing account, omitting only the technical data on barometric pressures, water temperatures, wind direction and the like.

1936: Snowshoed into Flopper's Pond with Clarence Lott. Pond partly open. No rises, no fish, no errors. Two flat tires on way out. "Oh, what fun it is to run . . ."

1937: Same way to same place with Mike DeFant. Reluctantly kept five wizened fryers out of low peasant pride.

1938: Slugged into Werner Creek beaver dam with mudhooks on Model A. Same fellows plus brother Leo. Caught 3 small trout and a touch of double pneumonia.

1939: Hiked into Wilson Creek beaver dams on snowshoes with Bill Gray. No rises, no takers. Bill took 6 fryers on bait. Spent balance of day coaxing the old fish car back across broken bridge. Finally did it with oats soaked generously in rum.

1940: Louis Bonetti, Nes Racine and Leo and I to O'Neil's Creek dam. A beautiful day succeeded by an even more beautiful hangover. No rises, no fish, several errors.

1941: Tom Cole and Vic Snyder and I drove out to the "Old Ruined Dams." Roads open, ponds free of ice. Fair rise. Beautiful day. Tom (6), Vic (7) and I (9), all honest fryers. All day long wedges of

geese honking over like crazy, sounding remarkably like the weirdly demented yowlings of a distant pack of coyotes.

1942: Same gang plus Leo, to same place, same conditions. I kept 5 fryers. Vic filled out on bait. Had fish fry that night in camp. Lost $2.50 at rum. Tossed and turned all night.

1943: (No fish and no entry of just where I went. My, my. Must have gone straight up! Maybe no gas coupons.)

1944: South camp with usual opening gang. Bucked drifts last 2 miles. High water. Picked arbutus on south hillsides. No fish in crowd. Drowned our sorrows in mead and wore twisted garlands of arbutus in our hair.

"RAINBOWS AND BEADHEAD"—MARK SUSINNO

1945: To Ted Fulsher's camp with Bill Gray and Carl Winkler. Raw, cold. Northeast wind. Didn't wet a line. Won $17.00 at poker. Slept like a log.

1946: To Frenchman's Pond with gang. Our fly lines froze in the guides. Thawed lines and drove to South Camp where Leo broke out a bottle of rare old brandy. Evidently it was *too* old: after the third round I suddenly rose and clapped my hand to my mouth—and ran outside. Guess I better stick to the reliable brands of medium rare one-year-old cookin' whisky, the kind designed for peasants of distinction—bent on extinction.

1947: Snowshoed 5 miles with Dick Tisch in to Nurmi's Pond. Snow still 3 feet deep in woods. Got caught in bitter cold mixed rain and snow. Came down with chills and vapors and spent three days with a nurse. Enervating but fun. Must try same next year. Her name was Lulu.

1948: Chopped way through the winter's bountiful supply of windfalls into O'Leary's Pond with Gipp Warner and Tom Bennett. Saw 2 wobbly young bear cubs and 17 deer. Caught 2 nice trout right off bat. Chuckled mirthlessly and twirled my waxed mustaches. Then caught in sudden hailstorm, which ended all fishing. On to Birchbark Lodge, one of those quaint Paul Bunyanish roadside tourist-traps cluttered to the eaves with stuffed owls and yawning dead bass impaled on varnished boards—and possessing the cutest iddy bitty bar, made, we

"UPRIVER"–PACO YOUNG

were solemnly assured, out of *real logs*. Next morning, snug in my doghouse, I suspected the whisky was, too.

1949: Snowshoed into Scudder's Pond with Joe Parker. Pond partly open over bubbling springs. Fish dimpling. Stood on ice and took 8 on tiny dry flies! 'Twas a miracle. Skidded them over the ice. *Skidding at Scudder's!* by George Bellows. . . . Joe took only 1 on spinning gear, the wrong medicine.

1950: To Alger County with Marquette gang. Felt like a midget. Out of seven men I was the shortest, at six feet. A tall tale! Snow, ice and high water everywhere. Didn't wet a line. Wet whistle instead. Excursion degenerated into a pub crawl. Lost count after the 17th. Heard 8 million polkas and hillbilly laments—all miraculously sung through the left nostril. Love and despair, your smell is everywhere. . . . The inventor of the juke box is a cross between a banshee and a fiend. May he and his accomplices roast in the bottommost pits of Hell.

1951: Slugged way through deep snow into Scudder's Pond led by proud Expedition Commander Frank Russell and his new jeep. The man *searched* for snowdrifts to charge! There is a new form of lunacy abroad in the land, the victims of which are called Jeepomaniacs. They're afraid of nothing. . . . Pond ice locked as tight as a bull's horns, as the saying doesn't go. Al Paul caught 2 in outlet—trout, not bull's horns. Surprise-attacked by party of

friendly natives. Entire expedition got half shot and retired in vast disorder.

1952: Mud-hooked way into Frenchman's Pond with Hank Scarffe and 2 boats. Nice intermittent "business" rise. Hank and I filled out, carefully selecting our trout. Fish fat and sassy. One of the most dramatic first-day rises I ever recall. Had but 2 bottles of beer all day. La, such a fine, contrite broth of a boy. Funny thing, I become a hell of a good fisherman when the trout decide to commit suicide. This is truly a fascinating pond.

And here is a later entry:

There have been 4 hauntingly lovely days in a row, the earth smoky and fragrant with the yeast of spring, the sky cut by the curling lash of endless flights of honking geese. Last night the wind swung abruptly to the east and the thermometer and barometer joined hands in a suicidal nose dive. Hank Scarffe, Al Paul, and I set out in 34° weather, the rainy sleet freezing to the windshield upon landing. All plans awry, we foolishly tried to reach the Moose Creek beaver dams, but got stuck up to the radiator in the first charge of a drift. We then retreated west and pushed and slugged our way through acres of rotten snow into Frenchman's Pond, where Hank and I huddled like wet robins and watched Al and his new telescope girder vainly test the pond with worms. Then came the snow, and there were *whitecaps* on the pond! Al folded his girder and we looked at each other and shrugged and slunk silently away. No one proposed even a drink. Once home I drained the fish car radiator, took a giant slug of whisky, and leapt morosely into bed, pulling the covers over my head. There I remained until nightfall, dreaming uneasily that I was a boy again and lo, it was Christmas—and I had just found my stocking filled with coal. I awoke to hear the blizzard screaming insanely outside. "*Whee-e-e . . .*" I crept downstairs in my bathrobe and drew every shade in the place, lit a roaring fire in the Franklin stove, built a foot-high highball, put on a mile-long piano concerto by Delius, and settled down with a book about hunting in Africa by a guy named, of all things, John A. Hunter. There were no pictures of fish! Was charmed to learn that the pygmies of Ituri forest cure eye infections by urinating in the bad eye. Found myself wishing that the red-eyed weather man would just sorta kinda drop in. Ho hum, only 8 more months 'til' Christmas.

But enough of this dreary recital of frustration, hangover, and rue. As you may by now suspect, the first day of fishing in my bailiwick is something of a gamble. Usually it is considerably more devoted to drinking than fishing, a state of affairs against which I maintain a stern taboo when the fishing really gets under way. *Then* any drinking—usually a nightcap or two—come only *after* the fishing is over and done. To me fly fishing is ordinarily quite difficult and stimulating enough without souping up the old motor. . . . But the first day is different; it is mostly a traditional spring get together of congenial souls, an incidental opportunity to

"JACK'S EMERGENCE—BROWN TROUT"–MARK SUSINNO

try out and find the bugs in one's equipment, and a chance to stretch one's legs and expand one's soul. I regret that it also frequently affords an excellent opportunity to entrench oneself early and firmly in the doghouse. Then comes the time for all middle-aged fisherman to sow their rolled oats. All of which brings on a final seizure of dubious poetry.

> *'Twas the morning after the first day*
> *When all through the house*
> *Echoed the moaning and groaning*
> *Of poor daddy—the louse!*

✦ The Last Day

Each year it is the same: this time, we tell ourselves, the doze and stitch and murmur of summer can never end; this season time will surely stand still in its tracks. Yet the hazy and glorious days glide by on golden wings, and presently here and there the leaves grow tinted by subtle fairy paintbrushes and flash their red warnings of impending fall. Even the trout become more brilliant in hue and grow heavy and loaded with spawn. And then, lo, one day we tired fishermen drag ourselves abroad only to discover that the stricken summer has waned into colorful northern autumn, like a beautiful woman flushed with the fevers of approaching death. It is the last day of fishing; the annual hibernation is once again at hand.

To this fisherman, at least, with all of its sadness and nostalgia the end of fishing is not unmixed with a sense of relief and release. No more is one oppressed by the curious compulsion of the chase; no more the driving sense of urgency that fills the eyes of fishermen

with flecks of stardust shot through with mad gleams of lunacy. Reason is temporarily restored. The precious rods can now be leisurely gone over and stashed; the lines cleaned and stored; the boots hung up by their feet, and all the rest of the sad ritual. Yes, and with a little luck perhaps diplomatic relations can even be restored with those strange but vaguely familiar ladies with whom we have been oh so absently sharing our bedrooms all summer long.

For many years I have speculated on the precise nature of the drives that possess a presumably reasonable man and turn him into that quietly mad creature we call a fisherman. I am satisfied that it is not merely the urge to kill and possess. In fact I now think—like Messrs. Gilbert and Sullivan—that this has nothing to do with the thing, tra la, has nothing to do with the thing. Most fishermen I know are poor or indifferent hunters; as a class they are apt to be a gentle, tweedy, and chicken-hearted lot; and, let us admit it, they are frequently reflective and poky to the point of coma. But allowing for all this I sometimes wonder whether they are not a more atavistic and elemental crew than most of their fellow men—even more so than their bombarding second cousins, the hunters.

All hunters, unless they have got themselves too loaded with cookin' whisky, invariably first see their quarry and know precisely what it is, and then deliberately sight and hurl a projectile at it—bullet, arrow, rock or what you will—while the fisherman rarely "sees" his fish in this sense, but rather must expend endless ingenuity and patience in approaching and luring his game to its fate. And perhaps

most important, when he is successful he is in actual, pulsing, manual contact with his quarry through the extension of his hand that he calls his line. The real combat only *begins*, when he "shoots" his game, that is, sinks the barb. This, to me, marks fishing as at once a more subtle and yet basically more primitive pursuit than hunting, or selling cars or TV sets on time—or even excelling in the absorbing mysteries of corporate financing.

At this late hour I don't want to go in over my waders and poach on the preserves of the psychiatrists. Thank heaven I have never been encouched and so am not qualified to. But sometimes I wonder whether the wild urge to pursue and lure a fighting fish isn't connected somehow with the–er–sexual urges of the fisherman himself. My, my, I've up and said it! Many frustrated and neglected wives of fishermen will doubtless rise up at this point and shout hoarsely, "What sexual urges?" Hm, let us see, let us see. . . .

Under the beneficent glow of our present pale tribal customs courtship and marriage can get to be, so my runners inform me, a pretty drab and routine affair; and I divine as though in a dream that some men there are among us who doubtless rebel at constantly laying siege to an already conquered citadel; and unless they are going in for collecting blondes of assorted shades and varying degrees of moral rectitude, fishing and all that goes with it may be the one pursuit that permits them to vent their atavistic impulses and still preserve the tatters of their self-respect. I do not labor the point, but smile evilly and cast my lure tightly upon the troubled waters—and quietly rejoin the drabber subject of the Last Day, the sad refrain upon which I seem to have opened this swan song.

On the last day all fishermen are akin to pallbearers; worse yet, they are pallbearers at their own funerals. Going out on the last day is a job that has to be done, like burying the dead; but their hearts aren't in the enterprise and the day is apt to be ruined by a future that looms ahead as bleak and hopeless as the grave. They may comfort themselves for the ordeal and brace themselves for the purgatory of waiting by telling themselves that it is all for the best. The fisherman's last-day funeral litany is a foggily beautiful and self-deceiving thing and runs something like this: the fishing is no longer sporting; the fisherman himself is dog-tired; the rise can no longer be depended on; the spawn-laden trout are far too easy to catch; and to take them now is to bite off one's nose. Amen.

Yes, on the last day we fishermen can try as we may to incant ourselves into hilarity and acceptance, but our hearts are chilled and our minds are numb. For what fishermen really want is to go on fishing, fishing, fishing—yes, fishing forever into the great far blue beyond . . . . All that sustains us in our annual autumnal sorrow is the wry knowledge that spring is but two seasons removed. After all, we can sadly croak, it's *only* eight more months till the magic *First Day*!

Excerpted from
TROUT MADNESS

"DUPED—BROWN TROUT"–MARK SUSINNO

"DAD'S WADERS"–JOSEPH SULKOWSKI

"... whatever our other feelings, we always felt it fitting that,

when we saw him catch his last fish, we never saw the fish but only

the artistry of the fisherman."

A RIVER

RUNS THROUGH IT

Norman Maclean
1976

. . . AFTER I CAUGHT these two, I quit. They made ten, and the last three were the finest fish I ever caught. They weren't the biggest or most spectacular fish I ever caught, but they were three fish I caught because my brother waded across the river to give me the fly that would catch them and because they were the last fish I ever caught fishing with him.

After cleaning my fish, I set these apart with a layer of grass and wild mint.

Then I lifted the heavy basket, shook myself into the shoulder strap until it didn't cut any more, and thought, "I'm through for the day. I'll go down and sit on the bank by my father and talk." Then I added, "If he doesn't feel like talking, I'll just sit."

I could see the sun ahead. The coming burst of light made it look from the shadows that I and a river inside the earth were about to appear on earth. Although I could as yet see only the sunlight and not anything in it, I knew my father was sitting somewhere on the bank. I knew partly because he and I share many of the same impulses, even to quitting at about the same time. I was sure without as yet being able to see into what was in front of me that he was sitting somewhere in the sunshine reading the New Testament in Greek. I knew this both from instinct and experience.

Old age had brought him moments of complete peace. Even when we went duck hunting and the roar of the early morning shooting was over, he would sit in the blind wrapped in an old army blanket with his Greek New Testament in one hand and his shotgun in the other. When a stray duck happened by, he would drop the book and raise the gun, and, after the shooting was over, he would raise the book again, occasionally interrupting his reading to thank his dog for retrieving the duck.

The voices of the subterranean river in the shadows were different from the voices of the sunlit river ahead. In the shadows against the cliff the river was deep and engaged in profundities, circling back on itself now and then to say things over to be sure it had understood itself. But the river ahead came out into the sunny world like a chatterbox, doing its best to be friendly. It bowed to one shore and then to the other so nothing would feel neglected.

By now I could see inside the sunshine and had located my father. He was sitting high on the bank. He wore no hat. Inside the sunlight, his faded red hair was once again ablaze and again in glory. He was reading, although evidently only by sentences because he often looked away from the book. He did not close the book until some time after he saw me.

I scrambled up the bank and asked him, "How many did you get?" He said, "I got four or five." I asked, "Are they any good?" He said, "They are beautiful."

He was about the only man I ever knew who used the word "beautiful" as a natural form of speech, and I guess I picked up the habit from hanging around him when I was little.

"How many did you catch?" he asked. "I also caught all I want," I told him. He omitted asking me just how many that was, but he did ask me, "Are they any good?" "They are beautiful," I told him, and sat down beside him.

"What have you been reading?" I asked. "A book," he said. It was on the ground on the other side of him. So I would not have to bother to look over his knees to see it, he said, "A good book."

Then he told me, "In the part I was reading it says that the Word was in the beginning, and that's right. I used to think water was first, but if you listen carefully you will hear the words are underneath the water."

"That's because you are a preacher first and then a fisherman, "I told him. "If you ask Paul, he will tell you that the words are formed out of the water."

"No," my father said, "you are not listening carefully. The water runs over the words. Paul will tell you the same thing. Where is Paul anyway?"

I told him he had gone back to fish the first hole over again. "But he promised to be here soon," I assured him. "He'll be here when he catches his limit," he said. "He'll be here soon," I reassured him, partly because I could already see him in the subterranean shadows.

My father went back to reading and I tried to check what we had said by listening. Paul was fishing fast, picking up one here and there and wasting no time in walking them to shore. When he got directly across from us, he held up a finger on each hand and my father said, "He needs two more for his limit."

I looked to see where the book was left open and knew just enough Greek to recognize—as the Word. I guessed from it and the argument that I was looking at the first verse of John. While I was looking, Father said, "He has one on."

It was hard to believe, because he was fishing in front of us on the other side of the hole that Father had just fished. Father slowly rose, found a good-sized rock and held it behind his back. Paul landed the fish, and waded out again for number twenty and his limit. Just as he was making the first cast, Father threw the rock. He was old enough so that he threw awkwardly and afterward had to rub his shoulder, but the rock landed in the river about where Paul's fly landed and at about the same time, so you can see where my brother learned to throw rocks into his partner's fishing water when he couldn't bear to see his partner catch more fish.

Paul was startled for only a moment. Then he spotted Father on the bank rubbing his shoulder, and Paul laughed, shook his fist at him, backed to shore and went downstream until he was out of rock range. From there he waded into the water and began to cast again, but now he was far enough away so we couldn't

see his line or loops. He was a man with a wand in a river, and whatever happened we had to guess from what the man and the wand and the river did.

As he waded out, his big right arm swung back and forth. Each circle of his arm inflated his chest. Each circle was faster and higher and longer until his arm became defiant and his chest breasted the sky. On shore we were sure, although we could see no line, that the air above him was singing with loops of line that never touched the water but got bigger and bigger each time they passed and sang. And we knew what was in his mind from the lengthening defiance of his arm. He was not going to let his fly touch any water close to shore where the small and middle-sized fish were. We knew from his arm and chest that all parts of him were saying, "No small one for the last one." Everything was going into one big cast for one last big fish.

"PLUNGE POOL—BROOK TROUT"—MARK SUSINNO

From our angle high on the bank, my father and I could see where in the distance the wand was going to let the fly first touch the water. In the middle of the river was a rock iceberg, just its tip exposed above water and underneath it a rock house. It met all the residential requirements for big fish—powerful water carrying food to the front and back doors, and rest and shade behind them.

My father said, "There has to be a big one out there."

I said, "A little one couldn't live out there."

My father said, "The big one wouldn't let it."

My father could tell by the width of Paul's chest that he was going to let the next loop sail. It couldn't get any wider. "I wanted to fish out there," he said, "but I couldn't cast that far."

Paul's body pivoted as if he were going to drive a golf ball three hundred yards, and his arm went high into the great arc and the tip of his wand bent like a spring, and then everything sprang and sang.

Suddenly, there was an end of action. The man was immobile. There was no bend, no power in the wand. It pointed at ten o'clock and ten o'clock pointed at the rock. For a moment the man looked like a teacher with a pointer illustrating something about a rock to a rock. Only water moved. Somewhere above the top of the rock house a fly was swept in water so powerful only a big fish could be there to see it.

Then the universe stepped on its third rail. The wand jumped convulsively as it made contact with the magic current of the world. The wand tried to jump out of the man's right hand. His left hand seemed to be frantically waving good-bye to a fish, but actually was throwing enough line into the rod to reduce the voltage and ease the shock of what had struck.

Everything seemed electrically charged but electrically unconnected. Electrical sparks appeared here and there on the river. A fish jumped so far downstream that it seemed outside the man's electrical field, but, when the fish had jumped, the man had leaned back on the rod and it was then that the fish toppled back into the water not guided in its reentry by itself. The connections between the convulsions and the sparks became clearer by repetition.

When the man leaned back on the wand and the fish reentered the water not altogether under its own power, the wand recharged with convulsions, the man's hand waved frantically at another departure, and much farther below a fish jumped again. Because of the connections, it became the same fish.

The fish made three such long runs before another act in the performance began. Although the act involved a big man and a big fish, it looked more like children playing. The man's left hand sneakily began recapturing line, and then, as if caught in the act, threw it all back into the rod as the fish got wise and made still another run.

"He'll get him," I assured my father.

"Beyond doubt," my father said. The line going out became shorter than what the left hand took in.

When Paul peered into the water behind him, we knew he was going to start working the fish to shore and didn't want to back into a hole or rock. We could tell he had worked the fish into shallow water because he held the rod higher and higher to keep the fish from bumping into anything on the bottom. Just when we thought the performance was over, the wand convulsed

"BROOK TROUT"
—ALAN JAMES ROBINSON

and the man thrashed through the water after some unseen power departing for the deep.

"The son of a bitch still has fight in him," I thought I said to myself, but unmistakably I said it out loud, and was embarrassed for having said it out loud in front of my father. He said nothing.

Two or three more times Paul worked him close to shore, only to have him swirl and return to the deep, but even at the distance my father and I could feel the ebbing of the underwater power. The rod went high in the air, and

the man moved backwards swiftly but evenly, motions which when translated into events meant the fish had tried to rest for a moment on top of the water and the man had quickly raised the rod high and skidded him to shore before the fish thought of getting under water again. He skidded him across the rocks clear back to a sandbar before the shocked fish gasped and discovered he could not live in oxygen. In belated despair, he rose in the sand and consumed the rest of momentary life dancing the Dance of Death on his tail.

The man put the wand down, got on his hands and knees in the sand, and, like an animal, circled another animal and waited. Then the shoulder shot straight out, and my brother stood up, faced us, and, with uplifted arm proclaimed himself the victor. Something giant dangled from his fist. Had Romans been watching they would have thought that what was dangling had a helmet on it.

"That's his limit," I said to my father.

"He is beautiful," my father said, although my brother had just finished catching his limit in the hole my father had already fished.

This was the last fish we were ever to see Paul catch. My father and I talked about this moment several times later, and whatever our other feelings, we always felt it fitting that, when we saw him catch his last fish, we never saw the fish but only the artistry of the fisherman. . . . At the end of this day, then, I remember him both as a distant abstraction in artistry, and a closeup in water and laughter.

My father always felt shy when compelled to praise one of his family, and his family always felt shy when he praised them. My father said, "You are a fine fisherman."

"FISHING THE FRYING PAN"–JOSEPH SULKOWSKI

My brother said, "I'm pretty good with a rod, but I need three more years before I can think like a fish."

Remembering that he had caught his limit by switching to George's No. 2 Yellow Hackle with a feather wing, I said without knowing what I said, "You already know how to think like a dead stone fly."

We sat on the bank and the river went by. As always, it was making sounds to itself, and now it made sounds to us. It would be hard to find three men sitting side by side who knew better what a river was saying. . . .

Of course, now I am too old to be much of a fisherman, and now of course I usually fish the big waters alone, although some friends think I shouldn't. Like many fly fishermen in western Montana where the summer days are almost Arctic in length, I often do not start fishing until the cool of the evening. Then in the Arctic half-light of the canyon, all existence fades to a being with my soul and memories and the sounds, of the Big Blackfoot River and a four-count rhythm and the hope that a fish will rise.

Eventually, all things merge into one, and a river runs through it. The river was cut by the world's great flood and runs over rocks from the basement of time. On some of the rocks are timeless raindrops. Under the rocks are the words, and some of the words are theirs.

I am haunted by waters.

Excerpted from
A RIVER RUNS THROUGH IT

"THE FLY WALLET"–JOSEPH SULKOWSKI

"Although I had fished for bass, bream, catfish,

and other warm-water fish since I was a child . . . there is something special

about fly-fishing for trout . . . a world of cold and pure flowing water,

rocks and waterfalls, personal solitude . . ."

NOTES *of a*

FLY-FISHERMAN

Jimmy Carter
1988

I DIDN'T NEGLECT my fishing in the Navy, but now that I've learned more about the different opportunities, it is obvious that I missed a lot.

I remember once when I was on the bridge of the U.S.S. *Pomfret*, a World War II submarine, we were cruising on the surface of the Pacific Ocean late at night, hundreds of miles from the nearest land. I was bored and struggling to stay awake until another of the ship's officers would relieve me. All of a sudden I was struck a heavy and painful blow on my right arm which both amazed and frightened me. I couldn't image what had hit me, until I heard something flopping around on the deck at my feet. It was a large flying fish, about sixteen inches long. The two lookouts and I had quite a discussion about this phenomenon, since we had never seen a fish flying so high—some fifteen feet above the surface.

The next morning I talked it over with the captain, who gave us permission to rig up a net and electric light on the main deck, only about three feet above the glassy-smooth water. The sailors and I had a good time catch-ing a couple of dozen fish. Then the cooks filleted them and gave us one of the best meals I've ever had at sea.

In more orthodox fashion, I fished many times for striped bass along the New England coast. My usual fishing partner was the submarine's hospital man, whose name was Blackmon. He and I used casting rods to fish from the Connecticut and Rhode Island breakwaters or jetties at night, sometimes from midnight until daybreak, with artificial lures or small eels for bait. Since it was often freezing cold and our lines were stiff, we were constantly plagued with backlashes that almost defied untangling in the dark with our frozen fingers.

It was then, in the late 1940s, that we first learned about spinning reels. Both of us promptly bought them; we fashioned our own Fiberglas rods and then were able to make long casts, with rare backlashes. Sometimes we rented or borrowed a small boat and trolled in the Thames River near New London. We caught a lot of fish, the largest one an eighteen-pound striper that Blackmon landed.

Rosalynn and I live in South Georgia in the Coastal Plains region, which was formerly covered by the Atlantic Ocean. Its climate is balmy, the landscape relatively flat, annual rainfall about fifty inches, and the farming regions highly productive. There is a tremendous aquifer underneath our land, with many millions of gallons of water moving very slowly up from the south, then turning eastward and emptying into the sea, taking thousands of years for any particular drop of water to complete the journey. Numerous springs well up from the ground to form our streams. Good drinking water can often be found in shallow dug wells; I remember that most of the open wells of my boyhood were only about twenty feet deep.

The streams run slowly in the level land, and it doesn't take the warm sun long to heat the water to a moderate temperature. Despite our other blessings, therefore, we southern fishermen have to go farther north to find such cold-water species as trout, salmon, char, or grayling. This is why, in spite of years of experience in warm-water lakes and creeks, I was still somewhat piscatorially retarded when we moved to Atlanta and the governor's mansion, just a few miles from the frigid waters of the Chattahoochee River. I soon asked Jack Crockford, director of Georgia's Game and Fish Department, to introduce me to the fly rod and trout fishing. Not only did we enjoy fishing the river from the shore, canoes, and floating tubes, but Rosalynn and I found time to sample some of the smaller streams in the North Georgia mountains.

Since this was one of the most gratifying developments of my life, when I was President I sought out opportunities to continue the sport. Early in my term our family took a delightful raft trip down the Middle Fork of the Salmon River in Idaho, fishing as we traversed one of the most beautiful scenic regions of our country. Later, when we watched some of the movies made of the voyage, I was distressed by my poor style, particularly when I attempted a longer cast. Rosalynn and I resolved to learn more about this exciting pastime.

Although I had fished for bass, bream, catfish, and other warm-water fish since I was a child, and still enjoy it just as much as ever, there is something special abut fly-fishing for trout. By taking up this sport fifteen years ago, I entered a world of cold and pure flowing water, rocks and waterfalls, quiet streams often nestled in meadows of mint and wild flowers, cool mountain valleys, personal solitude, and the exquisite science of imitating and presenting a myriad of sometimes tiny insects that comprise the elusive trout's diet.

There is also the enigma of the individual trout's habits and preferences; when I find him zealously feeding, he will totally reject any fly I offer to him, no matter how similar it might seem to those he is taking or how naturally it floats down and past him. I have come to realize over the years that close observation and patience are prerequisites for success. My eagerness to wade out into the current, or just to get a hook in the water, is most often best suppressed while a painstaking analysis of a stream is made: its depth, main flow-path, eddies, submerged obstructions, shadows on the surface, flotsam going by, overhanging banks and foliage. Only then am I able to make an educated guess about where fish might be lying, or perhaps actually sight an unwary quarry, all without revealing my presence by movement, shadow, or sound.

Fortunately for us modern-day fisherman, beginning a little more than a hundred years ago the eggs and fry of three major species of trout were transferred internationally to distant streams—brookies and rainbows from the Americas and browns from Europe. Now, with proper habitat, the introduced trout are thriving and even believed by many nonhistorians to be native to the area.

East. I have caught them in the smaller, more inaccessible streams of Maryland, Virginia, Pennsylvania, and a few in North Georgia, but always carefully released them in hopes that their population might increase. Like the browns and rainbows, brook trout have been introduced in many other areas in the world. Very large brook trout, in the ten-pound class, can still be caught in eastern Canada and in

"ORANGE HUMPY"–ROCK NEWCOMB

The only trout originally found in the eastern states was *Salvelinus fontinalis*, known as brook trout. Requiring water that is both pure and cold and being somewhat gullible when presented an attractive fly imitation, this most beautiful species has become almost extinct in many of the major streams of the

Argentina. The world record, caught on rod and reel, is fourteen pounds.

Rainbow trout, *Salmo gairdneri*, were originally native only to the Pacific coast but were brought to the eastern states in 1874. Today there are few cold and clear streams in the United States where rainbows cannot be

Adriano Manocchia

found. Rosalynn and I have also fished for them in New Zealand, Japan, and Switzerland. These fish are more hardy than the brookies, a little more cautious about taking artificial lures, and are spectacular fighters and leapers when hooked. However, rainbow trout are wanderers, tending to leave smaller streams where introduced and to move downstream until turned back by warm water or pollution. Migratory rainbows, known as steelhead, are extraordinary fighting fish. Like Atlantic Salmon, they spend a great part of their life in large lakes or the ocean, returning several times to their native streams to spawn. The largest steelhead caught on rod and reel weighed forty-two pounds.

Rosalynn and I have fly-fished for several other species, including lake trout, cutthroat trout in western streams, and grayling in the Yellowstone area, Alaska, England, and continental Europe. Grayling require the coldest and purest of waters and are seldom found in our country except in Alaska. The largest ever caught weighed six pounds.

The enormous size of record fish can be quite misleading. It is entirely possible for an expert to fish for a lifetime on the more popular streams of our country and never catch a trout that weighs as much as three pounds. In most areas, trout are measured by length, with fish just fifteen or sixteen inches being a source of pride. The smaller mountain streams often produce mature native trout of eight to twelve inches. In remote areas of Alaska, Canada, New Zealand, and Argentina, the fish are likely to be much larger, and fisherman are increasingly protecting these trophy trout from being killed. When caught they are handled carefully, photographed, and released to reproduce or perhaps to be caught again.

There is no way to understand tales about fly-fishing without knowing something about what trout like to eat. I have spent many hours studying the life cycles of the food prevalent in our fishing waters. There are three orders of stream insects that provide the basis for trout survival: mayflies, stoneflies, and caddis flies. It is not necessary in this book to describe the differences among them, but any successful fisher for trout would have to know. These aquatic insects share some common character-

"WORKING THE HATCH—RAINBOW TROUT"–MARK SUSINNO

istics that help to explain the fishing methods used to catch trout on a fly rod.

They are born from tiny eggs that hatch on the bottom of lakes and streams, protected by trash or rocks from the many predators that seek them for food. As nymphs, the insects then live for a year in their native water, successively shedding their protective shells up to twenty times as they increase in size. Some move quite rapidly and others slowly. When mature, the nymphs swim to the surface or crawl out on the shore, emerge from their last shell, unfold their wings after a few seconds and, when dry enough, fly into nearby trees and bushes to finish drying and sometimes to undergo another metamorphosis.

After a day or two, these winged insects gather in large numbers above the water, flying up and down in their aerial mating dance. Having copulated, the female swoops down to deposit her fertilized eggs in the water, and then this generation, male and female, dies as the eggs sink to the bottom to begin another cycle. These final stages of life, between the water and the air, are known as hatches, and often the trout go into a frenzy of feeding when the succulent insects are most prevalent and vulnerable. In well-populated pools I have often seen several dozen trout feeding simultaneously. At other times a single trout may be the only one periodically surfacing to feed. The challenge for a fly-fisherman is to recognize the particular insect that is hatching and, with a reasonable imitation, present the artificial fly to the feeding trout in a natural and believable fashion.

Sometimes mayflies hatch in enormous quantities. In August 1980, Rosalynn and I took a delightful voyage down the Mississippi River on an old paddle-wheeler, the Delta Queen, from St Paul, Minnesota, to St. Louis, Missouri. I spent a number of hours on the bridge with the captain, discussing steamboat history and the various points of interest along the shore. All around us, mayflies were hatching in unbelievable numbers. At times the captain had to keep the powerful window wipers going to remove the large adult insects that otherwise would have totally obscured our vision of the channel ahead. Each day, while the ship was traversing one of the many locks, I would get my exercise by running several miles either along the levees or across the dams that separated the river into successive downward steps to permit navigation. On one occasion, the pathway was covered at least two inches deep by the bodies of just-hatched mayflies. I wasn't sure, but they seemed to be what fly-fisherman call Light Gray Drake.

The hundreds of species of flies vary widely in size, from those much smaller than a mosquito to stoneflies as large as two inches in length, and in color from almost snow-white to black, with many yellows, goldens, browns, greens, and numerous shades of gray in between. For a particular pool or lake the hatches occur periodically; the date and times of day can be predicted by knowledgeable fishermen. Weather conditions cause variations of only a few days in the timing of hatches for a particular year. For instance, in our favorite Pennsylvania streams the caddis hatch will begin about April 15 and occur from 11:00am to 2:00pm; the Hendricksons come on May 1, starting each day around 2:00pm; the large Green Drake during the last days of May, almost simultaneously with the Sulfurs and

Light Cahills; and the tiny Tricorythodes will be hatching from July 20 until the end of the season, usually beginning when it warms up in the morning.

Once a hatch is on, the trout become highly selective, their metabolism quickly attuned to flies of a particular size, color, and configuration. Most often they will simply ignore those that deviate from this pattern. Many flies and nymphs, knows as midges, are almost too small to see, but for some unknown reason seem to be special favorites of the trout. One of the most frustrating and debilitating experiences of my sporting life is to present a dozen different imitations to feeding trout, all of which are totally ignored while they are regularly gulping down some unidentified and nearly invisible insect.

As can be surmised, about 75 percent of aquatic insects are consumed by trout in the long-lasting nymphal stage, and submerged fly imitations are undoubtedly the most effective way to catch fish. These are known either as wet flies or nymphs, depending on how the fly is made to travel underwater. The taking of the lure can be a vicious strike or so gentle as to be almost undetectable. For centuries, this subsurface presentation was the only one used, but in the nineteenth century in England the dry fly was introduced, a artificial fly that floats on the surface to imitate the emerging or hatching insect. This exciting new fishing technique was quickly adopted in our country, and is now by far our favorite way of fishing because the path of the floating fly can be followed (if it is large enough to see) and the taking of the lure by trout is visible and often explosive.

Of course, trout feed on many other morsels, including smaller fish, salmon roe and other eggs, frogs, worms, mice or moles, and a wide range of terrestrial insects that fall into the water. I have imitated all these in various ways, but the latter class—including crickets, beetles, jassids, grasshoppers, and ants of all sizes—provides one of the most important sources of dry fly patterns. In fact, if I had to go the rest of my fishing days with only one fly (heaven forbid!), I think I would choose a black ant imitation made of deer hair.

Fly-fishing at its best includes some of the elements of primal hunting: understanding the habitat of the trout, stalking an outstanding specimen while concealing your own presence, thoughtful assessment of what is always a unique situation, planning strategy, and intelligent execution of it with enough deception to prevail. Then perhaps a salute or apology to a worth adversary and—a significant difference—the ability to release the prey, unharmed.

Over the years I have accumulated an impressive library covering various aspects of fly-fishing, including information about aquatic insects and other trout food, how to tie artificial flies, and how to present the fly most attractively and seductively. I first set up my fly-tying vise and other paraphernalia in the room next to our bedroom in the White House that both Harry Truman and I also used as an office. Then, from my books, I learned how to create a few of the standard patterns.

Just down the mountain from Camp David was the small but well-stocked stream where Rosalynn and I found time during the weekend to catch a few trout. We also slipped away from presidential duties long enough to fish the upper reaches of the Potomac River for smallmouth bass, and explored trout streams in Maryland, Virginia, West Virginia, and southern Pennsylvania.

On one weekend at Camp David we invited about a dozen of the most notable fly-fishermen on the East Coast to visit. Rosalynn and I spent a delightful two days with them, discussing many of the aspects of the sport. A number of guests had written the books we read or were frequent contributors to the sporting magazines. We had a good program of slide shows, casting and fly-tying demonstrations, and lectures on trout habitat, conservation, and the history and customs of fly-fishing in various countries around the world. One of the highlights of the weekend was a demonstration by the Camp David chefs of how to fillet a trout, removing every bone and leaving the rest of the fish intact; they outdid themselves with some special recipes.

Shortly thereafter, we had an invitation from the Spruce Creek Hunting and Fishing Club for a day of fishing on a portion of their leased stream. This was only about as far north of Camp David as Washington was south of it, so we helicoptered in, to a field adjacent to the water. Our hosts met us, then graciously left us alone to fish. Before we left to return to civiliza-tion, Wayne Harpster, who owned the land, came to invite us to return at any time. So began one of the most cherished friendships of our lives. Thereafter, whenever it was possible, we went back to Spruce Creek, landed in Wayne's pasture near the stream, stayed overnight in an old but comfortable house, and enjoyed some of the best fishing in the eastern states.

These were the kinds of fishing expeditions Rosalynn and I squeezed into the interstices of a busy presidential life. They were always too brief but especially welcome. For a few hours we enjoyed the solitude we badly needed. Or, if we were fishing with expert companions, we were able to learn more and more about how to fish effectively under different conditions.

Since leaving the White House we have, predictably, found more opportunities to fish; we modify our busy schedules just enough to take advantage of them. After all these years, I still feel a lot like a boy when I'm on a stream or lake, enjoying the unique beauty of the moment, using all my wits and talents, making mistakes, catching a wily fish, and relishing the memories of bygone time.

Excerpted from
AN OUTDOOR JOURNAL

BAPTISM
of the
BROOK TROUT

R. H. Russell

1902

I am Salmo Fontinalis,
   to the sparkling fountain born,
And my home is where oxalis,
   Heather bell and rose adorn
     The crystal basin in the dell,
     (Undine the wood-nymph knows it well,)
     That is where I love to dwell.

There was I baptized and christened,
   'Neath the sombre aisles of oak,
Mute the cascade paused and listened,
   Never a word the brooklet spoke;
     Bobolink was witness then,
     Likewise Ousel, Linnet, Wren,
     And all the brownies joined "amen."

Noted oft in ancient story,
   Erst from immemorial time,
Poets, anglers, hermits hoary
   Confirm my vested rights sublime.
     All along the mountain range,
     "'Tis writ in mystic symbols strange:
     "Naught shall abrogate or change."

Thus as Salmo Fontinalis
   Recognized the wide world o'er,
In my limpid crystal palace,
   Content withal, I ask no more;
     Leaping through the rainbow spray,
     Snatching flies the livelong day.
     Naught to do but live and play.

Excerpted from
THE SPECKLED BROOK TROUT

Leaping through the rainbow spray,

Snatching flies the livelong day.

Naught to do but live and play.

"The whole idea of skill in casting, sound equipment and a good knowledge of

techniques is to free the mind for the pleasure of fishing. . .

but all these are the background of going fishing."

ETHICS

& AESTHETICS

Roderick Haig-Brown
1964

THERE IS, I THINK, not much point in being a fly-fisherman unless one is prepared to be generous and fairly relaxed about it all. Competition has no place at the streamside. One's purpose is not to do better than some other fisherman, but to get response from the fish and learn something about them, and both of these objectives are best achieved by the concentration of a relaxed mind.

The whole idea of skill in casting, sound equipment and a good knowledge of techniques is to free the mind for the pleasure of fishing. True, there is pleasure in casting, conscious pleasure in the proper use of techniques, even in the handling of good equipment, but all these are the background of going fishing. One enjoys them, whether the fish are there or not, but they should never intrude. If the skills have been mastered, if they are used naturally, almost instinctively, they will not intrude, but will simply provide greater freedom for enjoyment.

The generosity I am thinking of is an attitude, a whole approach to the whole subject. It implies generosity to other fishermen,

to the fish themselves, to the water and surroundings in which they live. It is something a fly-fisherman can well afford and, by affording it, add greatly to his pleasure and relaxation.

Generosity to other fishermen is, I suppose, no more than common courtesy, but it should be a matter of feeling as well as practice. On private waters where fishermen are few, this should come easily enough, but on public waters that are more or less heavily fished it may require rather more conviction. Yet the logic of "do as you would be done by" has even stronger application on public than on private waters.

The first courtesy should be to respect another fisherman's privacy—that is, to avoid crowding him, to give him room to follow through his normal fishing plan. On streams this means that one should avoid entering too closely below a fisherman who is working downstream or too closely above one working upstream; better still, enter below the man who is fishing upstream and above the one who is working down. On lakes it is wrong to crowd a boat out of its planned drift, to cut in ahead of a boat working the shoreline or to anchor too close to another anchored boat. To those who fish extremely crowded waters, these may seem impossible counsels, but in my experience they are not. An opening weekend or some other special occasion may make difficulties, but even at such times the tendency is to crowd certain particular places and the mildest of non-conformists can avoid these. If he does, he usually finds less cluttered water, perhaps of less repute, but at least as likely to yield a fish or two as any of the pestered pools. On more normal occasions it is often simply a matter of waiting and watching while a single fisherman, or at most two or three, fish through a pool. If they fish well, there is pleasure in watching them; if they fish badly there is the slightly less respectable pleasure of noting the likely places that are passed by; and in either event there is a surprisingly good chance of finding fish when one's own turn comes. I have fished a dry fly upstream all day while meeting an unending downstream flow of spinners, bait fishermen and wet-fly fishermen and still had a respectable catch to show for it.

On lakes it is much the same. One may not be able to get into some favorite spot or drift, but it can happen that one find an even more productive place as a result. Similarly, one can often wait out several fishermen who have anchored over a lively shoal, move in when they have gone and find plenty of fish there still. Angling at its most deadly is seldom such an efficient means of catching fish that nothing is left.

If one happens to be in fortunate possession of a pool or a good stretch of water when other fishermen arrive, the reasonable thing is to fish it out with care, but without unneces-sary delay or disturbance and surrender it promptly and graciously. Lasting friendships can be made in this way. If the new arrivals are unkind enough to push in immediately ahead, it is often possible to give them time to widen the gap and then work on successfully. If they happen to be static bait fishermen, the only thing is to go around, giving them a wide berth for their own activities. Only occasionally is the invasion so impossibly vigorous that there is nothing left but to reel in and move on.

It is ordinary water-side courtesy to give, freely and honestly, whatever assistance or

It is always an important courtesy to disturb the fish and the water as little as possible, so that any fisherman following behind will have a fair chance, and this obligation is redoubled on waters where fish are usually shy and sophisticated. A competent fly-fisherman should be able to put a succession of flies over a difficult fish and leave him still in position when he gives up.

This, perhaps, is also an expression of generosity to the fish. If one isn't good enough to take him, why disturb his pleasant affairs by clumsy persistence? But there are others, even more important. Of all fishermen, the fly-fisherman needs fewest fish to complete his day. To him, every fish taken should be an affair of interest. He can afford to be selective and usually his chosen method allows him to be selective. A limit, if there is one, should be a meaningless figure, except that it may not be exceeded. He may occasionally wish to take a limit of fish, if he has a use for them. More often two or three fish of good size will make his day. More than that will be a burden rather than a blessing. Occasionally he may prefer to kill no fish at all, but his sport need never suffer for this; he can catch a dozen if he wishes and return them all safely to the water, secure in the knowledge that if he uses reasonable care all are likely to survive to provide sport for someone else.

But if a fish is to be killed, it should be killed promptly and efficiently, by a smart rap on the base of the skull, not left to flop and flounder until it dies. And if a fish is to be returned to the water it should be freed with all possible care and an absolute minimum of handling. If, as very rarely happens with the fly, it is hooked deep in the gullet or if it is bleeding

advice another fisherman may ask for. Let him know if you have found a particular fly successful and offer him a sample if he has nothing like it. Tell him anything you know of the peculiarities of the lake or stream or of likely places to fish. Offer to help in netting a fish if the occasion arises. But remember, too, that in the matter of unsolicited advice, it is more generous to receive than to give. Unless it happens that your local knowledge is complete, your wisdom flawless and your particular piece of information certain to produce the desired result, it is better to wait to be asked for it.

heavily from a wound in the gills, it should probably not be returned.

Occasionally, on closely managed water, there may be a duty to kill fish for the good of the fishery. If so, it is a duty to be respected. But very few public waters indeed are so closely managed that killing fish is a necessity, and usually there are plenty of killers available anyway.

Yet this point does bring up the fisherman's final and most important obligation to the fish, which is to respect his environment, to protect it to the best of his ability and to fight for it if necessary, which it usually is. Good fishing is being destroyed all over North America and the destruction is always unnecessary. When streams and lakes are damaged it is almost invariably the result of bad planning and bad management in the use of other resources. Clean waters, unobstructed waters and undepleted waters are in the long-term interest of everyone; only the shortest of short-term interests are ever served by pollutions, however caused, by temporary diversions, by obstructions that do not allow for adequate fish passage or by the sort of land use that permits silting and causes floods in winter and low flows in summer. If he respects his sport, a fisherman will learn to understand such things and to make his voice clearly heard. There are few better ways of doing this than by actively supporting some local rod and gun club.

This respect for this fish's environment, in my own humble opinion, extends far beyond the water itself. It takes in all the creatures and growth under the water or on the water or along the banks. It extends far out into the countryside, into the meadows and swamps, up into the high mountains where the streams have their origin. It implies not merely a

"EVENING SHADOWS"—ADRIANO MANOCCHIA

concern for such things and a desire to protect them, but a positive affection for the whole natural world and a deep desire to understand it.

I have no wish, for instance, to consider such beautiful creatures as merganser and herons and water ouzels, otter and mink and bears competitive predators for my sport. They belong where they are, they have their place and part and it is very rarely indeed that some unnatural factor allows them to increase to an excessive abundance that needs control. I have no special urge to cut away brush and tree limbs that make casting more difficult, for I learned long ago that these often make the places that shelter the best fish.

Fishing is a sport and a relaxation because it offers a man the ideal means of self-realization through close and peaceful identification with his surroundings. Awareness is an important part of this, and so is understanding. Any fisherman needs to concentrate, a fly-fisherman perhaps more than most. But there is always a time to forget rod and line and fly and look at other things. It is time well spent, if understanding grows. Every bird and mammal, every insect and weed and tree that can be recognized and named is something added to a man's stature. Every link between them, every change of stream bed or flow, every little thing observed and understood adds to the self-realization, emphasizes the fisherman's identification with his special world. A large part of a fisherman's pleasure should be in these things. In making it so, he will make himself a better fisherman, even though he may kill fewer fish.

Excerpted from
A PRIMER OF FLY-FISHING

THE ANGLER'S SONG

Izaak Walton

1653

As inward love breeds outward talk,
The Hound some praise, and some the Hawk:
Some better pleas'd with private sport,
Use Tennis, some a Mistress court:
    But these delights I neither wish,
    Nor envy, while I freely fish.

Who Hunts, doth oft in danger ride;
Who Hawks, lures oft both far and wide;
Who uses Games, shall often prove
A loser; but who falls in love,
    Is fettered in fond Cupid's snare:
    My angle breeds me no such care.

Of recreation there is none
So free as fishing is alone;
All other pastimes do no less
Than mind and body both possess:
    My hand alone my work can do,
    So I can fish and study too.

I care not, I, to fish in seas,
Fresh rivers best my mind do please;
Whose sweet calm course I contemplate
And seek in life to imitate:
    In civil bounds I fain would keep,
    And for my past offences weep.

And when the timorous Trout I wait
To take, and he devours my bait,
How poor a thing sometimes I find
Will captivate a greedy mind:
    And when none bite, I praise the wise,
    Whom vain allurements ne'er surprise.

But yet, though while I fish I fast,
I make good fortune my repast,
And thereunto my friend invite,
In whom I more than that delight:
    Who is more welcome to my dish,
    Than to my angle was my fish.

As well content no prize to take,
As use of taken prize to make:
For so our Lord was pleased when
He fishers made fishers of men:
  Where, which in no other game,
  A man may fish and praise his name.

The first men that our Saviour dear
Did choose to wait upon him here,
Blest fishers were, and fish the last
Food was that he on earth did taste:
  I therefore strive to follow those,
  Whom he to follow him hath chose.

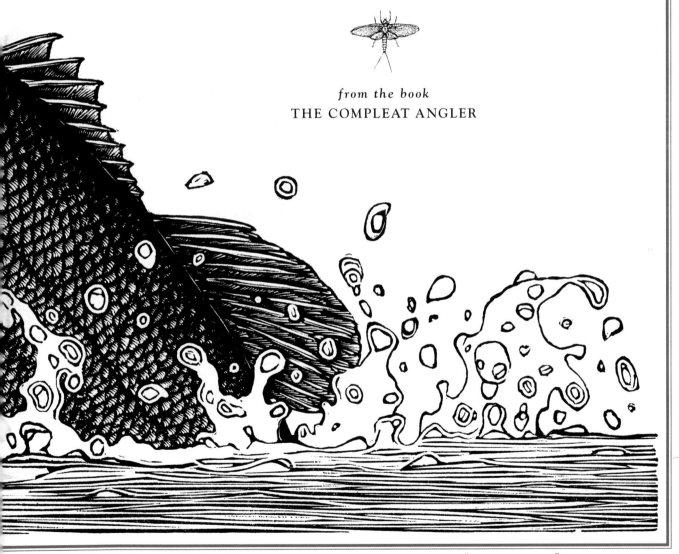

from the book
THE COMPLEAT ANGLER

"LARGEMOUTH BASS"–ALAN JAMES ROBINSON

Ode to Bass & Trout—Plates Listing